Authentically
ENGAGED
FAMILIES

For my husband, Kenneth, and our children, Autumn, Temple, Lauryn, and Leila. Without your love and support, this book would not have been possible.

Authentically ENGAGED FAMILIES

A Collaborative Care Framework for Student Success

Calvalyn G. Day

CORWIN
A SAGE Publishing Company

FOR INFORMATION:

Corwin

A SAGE Company

2455 Teller Road

Thousand Oaks, California 91320

(800) 233-9936

www.corwin.com

SAGE Publications Ltd.

1 Oliver's Yard

55 City Road

London EC1Y 1SP

United Kingdom

SAGE Publications India Pvt. Ltd.

B 1/I 1 Mohan Cooperative Industrial Area

Mathura Road, New Delhi 110 044

India

SAGE Publications Asia-Pacific Pte. Ltd.

3 Church Street

#10-04 Samsung Hub

Singapore 049483

Senior Acquisitions Editor: Jessica Allan

Senior Associate Editor: Kim Greenberg

Editorial Assistant: Katie Crilley

Production Editor: Jane Haenel

Copy Editor: Jocelyn Rau

Typesetter: C&M Digitals (P) Ltd.

Proofreader: Sue Irwin

Indexer: Kathy Paparchontis

Cover Designer: Scott Van Atta

Marketing Manager: Jill Margulies

Printed in the United States of America

Library of Congress Cataloging-in-Publication Data

Names: Day, Calvalyn G., author.

Title: Authentically engaged families : a collaborative care framework for student success / Calvalyn G. Day.

Description: Thousand Oaks, California : Corwin, a SAGE Company, 2016. | Includes bibliographical references and index.

Identifiers: LCCN 2015049643 | ISBN 9781506327068 (pbk. : alk. paper)

Subjects: LCSH: Home and school—United States. | Parent-teacher relationships—United States. | Education—Parent participation—United States.

Classification: LCC LC225.3 .D39 2016 | DDC 371.19/2—dc23

LC record available at http://lccn.loc.gov/2015049643

This book is printed on acid-free paper.

16 17 18 19 20 10 9 8 7 6 5 4 3 2 1

Contents

Publisher's Acknowledgments   vii

About the Author   ix

Introduction   1

1. Parent Engagement 101   11

2. Understanding Parents   23

3. Defining the Goals   49

4. Communication   55

5. Program Components   75

6. Expanding the Tools in Your Toolbox   101

7. Putting It All Together   119

References and Further Readings   137

Index   141

 Additional materials and resources related to *Authentically Engaged Families: A Collaborative Care Framework for Student Success* can be found at http://resources.corwin.com/DayAuthenticallyEngagedFamilies

Publisher's Acknowledgments

Corwin thanks the following reviewers:

Grace Francis
Assistant Professor of Special Education
George Mason University
Fairfax, VA

Nina Orellana
Title I/MTSS Coordinator
Palm Bay Academy Charter School
Palm Bay, FL

Joyce Stout, PhD
School Counselor
Redondo Beach Unified School District
Redondo Beach, CA

Denise Michelle Voelker, EdD
Coordinator of Education and Training Programs, College of Medicine
Lecturer, College of Education
University of Florida
Gainesville, FL

Rosemarie Young
Retired Principal, KAESP Executive Director
Kentucky Association of Elementary School Principals
Louisville, KY

About the Author

 **Calvalyn G. Day** achieved a bachelor's degree from Indiana University in 2011. She then received her master's of science in educational counseling from Indiana University in 2013. She currently practices as a parent coach with The Well Counseling and Consulting Group, focusing on supporting parents of children with anxiety and ADHD, and as a home-based therapist to families impacted by trauma, abuse, and neglect. In 2014, Calvalyn used her extensive experience working in and around schools for over 15 years to coauthor her first book, *Drag 'Em Kicking and Screaming: Your Seven-Step Action Plan for At-Risk Student Success*, and now provides consulting and coaching to professionals on subjects including parent engagement and trauma-sensitive teaching. Calvalyn is passionate about bridging the gap between school and home for all students. She has experience with special education, behavior improvement plans, and motivational interviewing.

Introduction

Growing up, I'm not sure that my parents came to my school more than twice a year. Once for the parent teacher conference or open house and once for the one time per year that I was either sick or injured and needed to go home. If you ask my mother, to this day, she will say that she NEVER helped me with my homework. She couldn't tell you the difference between the PTO, the PTA, or a UFO for that matter.

My parents worked hard. They both spent 40+ hours at work each week, volunteered regularly within the community and at our church, and were known around the neighborhood to be a good place to get a hot meal and a kind or inspiring word. They provided me with structure, discipline, and a foundation of faith and strong character.

If you were to present the first paragraph as a description of my parents to a group of educators, they would likely tell you that they have a room full of parents like this. You would probably hear words as kind as "absentee" or as harsh as "apathetic." You might even believe that my parents were unengaged, passive, or potentially neglectful. However, the second description paints the picture of upstanding community members: law-abiding, tax-paying, good-hearted family leaders. The inconsistency of perception of these portraits is one of the reasons why I desired to create this book.

Data on parent and family engagement are undeniable. The research on how effective engagement is in the overall success of children has been around for decades. Parents know they need to "help." Furthermore, a recent study conducted by NBC News Education Nation states that schools know that they need parents (NBC News Education Nation, 2014). Even so, there is a critical missing link. Educators are not taught to engage parents and parents are not taught to be teachers. The bridge between school and home has to be created, implemented, and maintained through a comprehensive approach to considering all perspectives and removing barriers to engagement.

The challenge is real.

Not only do most major universities do a poor job of providing undergraduate education majors with instruction on supporting positive parent and family engagement, with more pressure than ever being placed on schools to "perform," less money is spent on professionally developing these educators once they are teaching. Most professional development time is devoted to standard instructional methods and, perhaps, behavior management. Many educators enter the classroom either fearful of dreaded parent interactions or committed to working around parents, sure that they will never be supported the way that they need to be.

Parents, though they most often mean well, feel less equipped than ever to support schools. Common Core has thrown many parents for a loop, and the additional pressures of maintaining a home while living the American dream leave very little time, resources, or confidence for parents, even those who want to provide educators with the support for which they long. Beyond volunteering for a school field trip or selling a few fundraising items, many parents can feel ill-equipped for the task of educating their children.

On a recent evening, I entered the office of a school leader to be part of a case conference committee for a kindergarten student. I had known this student's mother for several months and was eager to have this meeting, because this student was making such strides. I had, and still have, nothing but hope for his future. My hopes were not always this strong, given that when I met him for the first time, his reputation had preceded him to the point where I recognized him simply by his refusal to come in from recess when I saw him from my office window.

His mother, who has three other children, two older and one younger, works third shift and started the meeting by saying that, at 4 p.m., she had yet to go to sleep from her last shift and would be beginning her next one in a couple of hours. I appreciated her honesty. She was tired. She was not dismissive of the process but was sharing her need in that moment. In true counselor fashion, I led with empathy, affirming how difficult it must be to function on no sleep and that I appreciated her willingness to be there. With no ill intention, a teacher in the room offered that this would be a long meeting, mainly because there was a lot to go over. I was surprised that she did not recognize that she was being dismissive, primarily because that is not her nature. But it is a clear example of how the process can get in the way of the progress. In that moment, our primary goal was to build the case conference committee team. Establishing a relationship is key to any successful team or group dynamics. Had we been speaking with a less supportive mother, I know that that statement could have cost us.

However, the relationship with this mom was strong and she brushed it off. Not only have I personally been to her home, meeting with her family, immediate and extended, but she also knows I care for her son and she has seen that he cares for me. Her son has struggled for years through day care, preschool, and a previous elementary school that "suggested" that she take her son home and not bring him back. Home life and family functions have been nearly impossible as well. Her belief that we have not given up on her son had bought us some grace.

As we got into the meeting, going through psychologist reports, assessments, and data, there was so much material to grasp. I interjected every once and a while to confirm that mom was still with us. I was pleasantly surprised each time that she was not only with us but had done her homework and read through all of the materials prior to the meeting. She came prepared with questions, none written, but as we reached each section where there was a question, she felt comfortable to ask.

Then we reached the point where you could tell that her understanding of all of her then-answered questions and the material that was placed before her, including the proposed individualized education plan, had sunk in. She asked the simple question, "Is he going to have to repeat kindergarten?"

This question was so simple. She wanted to know if her son would be able to keep up with his peers. The greater question is unspoken. She wanted to know about her son's future.

A few hesitant educators around the table not quickly responding "No" led her to continue.

"I mean, I just want him to take it seriously. If he has to repeat, it won't really hurt him. But I know he's smart and I just want him to be here and learn."

And there you have it.

What I have said from the beginning. What I know to be true. The basis for all that I do in my work with parents.

She has a dream for her son.

She wants what's best for her son.

She wants him to be successful.

She cares.

Now if you pulled this student's records and looked at them in black and white, you might disagree with me. You would see dozens, yes, dozens of absences. You would see no early interventions prior to kindergarten. You may even deem his home life as, shall we say, less than traditional.

Just like my first description of my parents, on paper, this mother looks like many marginally interested, minimally involved parents who drive educators up the wall.

But she cares.

This leads me to the essential, driving force behind this book. Contrary to the educational world years ago, the role of the modern-day educator has evolved, and a renovation of the approach to parent and family engagement must occur. Educators have to work harder to eliminate judgment and blame from tainting our perspective. We are tasked with undoing years of distrust and negative media attention that tints the view that many parents have of traditional educational models. To minimize, insult, or alienate parents, even when we feel that their behavior is negatively impacting the child, is a counterproductive task that has to stop. Much like a successful co-parenting relationship, our role must be to connect with the dream that the parent has for their child and use it to build a path, brick by brick, that will pave the way to our student's brightest future.

The process of undoing ineffective patterns of behaviors is a daunting one. Adapting a collaborative care approach designed by medical professionals to systematically produce productive behaviors is the foundation for this book. The following chapters will walk you step by step from initial evaluation of parent and family engagement efforts through enhancing program outcomes with sustainability in a format that will challenge, enlighten, and empower you. These tools have been battle tested on schools just like yours: poor, underperforming rural schools; thriving urban and suburban buildings; elementary, middle, and high schools; and unique combinations of multi-age-level buildings as well. Many face the same challenges that you do: shrinking budgets, low staff morale, and parents who are so jaded about education or overwhelmed by life that getting them engaged seems an impossible task.

I am reminded of a recent visit I made to the home of a client. Not having visited the home before, I typed the address into my GPS. I followed the directions turn by turn, right up to the moment where I was met with a road closed sign. According to my GPS, the house was literally within walking distance of this sign, yet I could not drive through. The construction extended itself in the most unfortunate pattern, making all through streets impassable. Finally, after re-navigating multiple times and coming from a completely different direction, I arrived at the house. I was angry that the client had not warned me about the dreadful construction that had wasted my time and my gas.

My GPS was not aware of the road closure. It did not take into account the roadblocks that I would encounter. My client, who likely did not generally take my path and who was familiar with the neighborhood in which she lived, did not think about the roadblock as a challenge. She knew how to navigate the path. She held the tools to navigate the journey but was unaware of the need to provide me with those details.

The following week when I returned for another visit, instead of using the map, I tried to retrace my steps using the landmarks that I had seen leaving the previous visit. With ease, I was able to identify that although two of the more common entry points to the street were blocked, there was a completely accessible entry point that brought me nearly effortlessly to the door. What I realized in this moment was that even though the path I thought I needed had been blocked, there was still a path that got me where I needed to be.

Modern education is often much like a trip to an unfamiliar address. We have a general idea of how to get where we need to go, even tools to use to get us there. We know our students need basic skills and we have a general idea about how to get them there, but with challenges like poverty, limited language, or family and social concerns, not to mention larger-scale problems like systemic racism, we feel like we have reached an insurmountable roadblock. The purpose of *Authentically Engaged Families: A Collaborative Care Framework for Student Success* is to provide you with not only a road map but more of a guided tour that takes into account the roadblocks and street closures that you may encounter, as well as shortcuts to make your trip easier.

By utilizing the collaborative care model, which has been effective for many years in the medical world, we have created a simple Vision, Plan, Action method to make this process both user-friendly and reproducible. In addition to my own experience in and around school buildings, after-school programs, and community organizations, I have also collaborated with several schools to test these theories ethnographically.

As a follow-up to my first story about the kindergarten student, let me add that while he has not graduated yet, the process yielded a diagnosis that prompted his mother to seek additional resources. She has advocated for him to have additional interventions and he is doing well.

A WORD ABOUT COLLABORATIVE CARE

I became aware of the collaborative care model while working in home-based therapy. My primary role was providing therapeutic interventions to families involved in Department of Children's Services (DCS) cases. As you can imagine, the needs are high. The stakes are higher, and often we are dealing with complex challenges and less than enthusiastic participants.

When a family has entered the "system," they are given a caseworker in the DCS office. Then they will most often be given a therapist, a home-based case manager, a social worker, a guardian ad litem for the children, and even more. If the children are removed from the home, there will be foster or relative caregiver placements and a set of providers for them as well. All of these people coordinate with the original DCS caseworker to make sure that the family gets the support that they need. In the behavioral health industry, collaborative care has been widely recognized as one of the most effective models of managing the treatment of patients with complex mental health needs. Particularly, when working with patients who are impacted by multiple diagnoses, limited resources, or other extenuating circumstances, the collaborative care model pushes for an "all hands on deck approach."

In my communication with many educators, especially those who believe in providing support services to students and families, they often struggle with identifying where to draw the line. Things like scope of practice, experience, and even just time management can make it very difficult for anyone to feel like they are making the progress that they need to make. Traditionally, the relationship between parents and families and schools is more hierarchal in that the school is seen as the authority. The collaborative care model brings all the players to the table and allows us to identify strengths and challenges proactively with a team approach.

Traditionally, there are a minimum of three roles on the collaborative care team: one being a primary care physician, one being case management personnel, and a consultant who is aware of the needs of this particular patient and has a specialized set of skills for providing care. The benefits in the mental health world are amazing. Things like decreased depression and reduced need for medication have led to recommendations for this model to be the practice of choice. It can be more cost-effective, and all participants feel more supported, which leads to better results.

In many instances, however, the team is much larger. The multidisciplinary nature of the team allows for a variety of "experts" to impact individual patients on a deeper level. There can be therapists, specialists, and advocates who also contribute. The idea is that if we all come to the table, tell what we know, and use our individual strengths, we can all make the most of the time we have with the patient. By sharing information with each other, there can be a greater ability to make connections with the patient as well, helping to eliminate duplication and saving time.

Using the collaborative care framework as a guide, each student would essentially become the "patient." Parents are in the role of primary care physician, and teachers become case managers. Support personnel like counselors, aids, and others are consultants, utilize their knowledge of the student and his or her needs to positively impact conversations. When we look at parent and family engagement under this model, it changes drastically. We go from telling parents what *we* need from them to having honest conversations about what our students need from the "team." In Figure I.1, you will see a visual representation of the collaborative care approach to engaging families.

My theory is that by taking on some of the attributes of this approach, we can apply them to the way we advocate for student success. By implementing the spirit of collaborative care into the framework of the school, this approach will remove the "us" and "them" of the current educational model and take on the true team approach, with less concern for roles and more attention to outcomes.

If you think about it, this makes perfect sense in an educational setting. For example, if you have worked in special education for any length of time, collaborative care may feel familiar. In many ways, a similar approach comes into play with students who have an Individualized Education Plan (IEP). The system of assessing students on multiple facets then bringing together all the stakeholders has been shown to be an effective method of supporting the complex dynamics associated with students who have special education needs.

In terms of parent engagement, each family is indeed its own system. We have students who come to us to learn a variety of things, academics,

Figure I.1 The Collaborative Care Framework

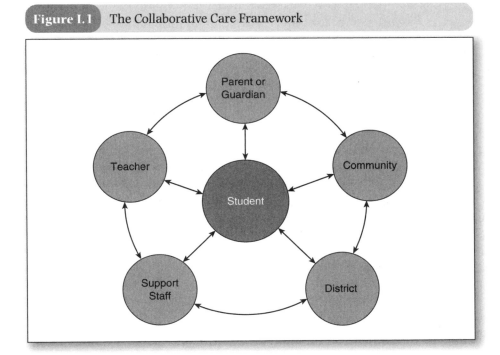

social skills. and emotional development. Some come with a strong foundation, others with no preparation at all. Ultimately, teachers are tasked with teaching children and providing the instruction that will take them from where they are to where they need to be, but expecting the teacher to do it alone is ludicrous. Parents bring their children to us to facilitate learning. Integrating the needs of the student and family with the goals of the teachers and school was described by one writer as an intricate dance in that it requires knowledge of technique with personalized artistic flair. The traditional model of parent engagement, where schools provide standard resources to all families and request certain behaviors in return, does very little to establish a team atmosphere that is specialized for individuals.

THE VISION, PLAN, ACTION METHOD

Throughout this book, you will see me refer to VPA; this stands for vision, plan, and action. The Vision, Plan, Action model for approaching parent engagement is a general approach to hold ourselves accountable for the statements, decisions, and behaviors we exhibit when seeking to connect with families. While we work through the chapters of this book, I will ask you to self-reflect on each by addressing the following criteria:

- *Vision*—Create a shared, realistically achievable vision to be used as an anchor point for the formal engagement plan
- *Plan*—A formalized document with actionable points agreed upon by all stakeholders
- *Action*—Specific points of activity and behavior that can be monitored for accountability and effectiveness

The reflection questions will help lead you to the creation of a successful family engagement plan. By beginning with the end in mind and collaborating with stakeholders to create a shared vision, educators can effectively plan for the completion of activities that promote that vision and take on specific action points that can be easily monitored and adjusted for maximum success.

ABOUT THIS BOOK

Let me begin by saying that whenever you see the word "parent" in this book, it is taken to mean the person or persons in the position of parenting your student. At times, this may be a grandparent, sibling, extended family member, foster parent, or some combination of the previously mentioned family members. At times, I will use the term "parent and family" and at other times, simply "parent"; the terms are used interchangeably and are never meant to exclude anyone who may be providing care for your students.

This book is the culmination of years of research, a passion for supporting and empowering parents and families, and a desire to enhance the preparation of teachers who want to do the same. Because traditional teacher education programs in this country are doing a less than stellar job of preparing fledgling educators with the skills to effectively communicate and collaborate with parents, there is a great need to fill the gap for new hires. However, many seasoned educators are also yearning for a fresh approach, based on research but realistic in implementation. Most importantly, it comes from a place of wanting all students to be holistically supported as they develop their unique gifts and knowing that doing this effectively requires more than what we as educators can do alone.

This book is written from my perspective as a parent, counselor, and professional parent coach working with a variety of families in and out of school settings. Professional school counselors, social workers, teachers, administrators, Title I interventionists, and parent and teacher organizations will all find tools in this book that can impact practices and streamline systems of engaging families. This book can be used to guide the creation of a formal engagement plan or simply for individuals looking to add strategies to an existing plan. My goal with this book is to make the significant research available on parent and family engagement more user-friendly by highlighting ways in which I or other professionals have used it in tangible, practical ways.

Whenever I conduct a training session, write a blog, or even when I have general conversations in session with clients, it is my hope that I share both information and inspiration with whomever I encounter. This book is no different. If you have a thirst for information on engaging parents and families, there is a foundation of theory and basic practices. In this book, you will find that I spend just enough time on the overview of the standard material while providing the tools for further research if needed. As a practicing educator, I know many schools, particularly those with high needs, find much of the theoretically based material to be accurate but lacking concrete application techniques. My goal for this book is simple. If you are in a Title I school, alternative school, online school, or, like me, work in a school where 70 percent of your families speak a language other than your own, you will see some tips you possibly have not considered. My hope is that you have a new passion for connecting with families in spite of the challenges. My desire is that the tools here will save you a few late nights of research and prevent you from being frustrated by inconsistent results from practices that are not meeting your needs. But most importantly, my hope is that, with the help of this book, partnerships will be formed that leave all involved changed for the better.

The book is designed to walk you through all of the things you should consider when writing a formal parent engagement plan. While these plans are not necessarily required for schools, I believe that without a formal plan, schools are reduced to inconsistent random acts of engagement, which do very little to create the team atmosphere that we want with ALL families. Throughout this book, you will find templates and examples, suggestions and ideas, and hopefully simple ways to take the abstract concepts of relationship building and make them more achievable. As often as possible, these ideas have been tested by me or other colleagues with whom I am fortunate enough to work; however, in full disclosure, there are a few that are currently on my wish list and have not been completed as of this publication. I recommend that you mark in this book, use the reflection questions to fine tune your vision and spark your imagination, and let this book be a tool that you use like a great cookbook. Take the "recipes" and add your own special touch so that your staff and families' needs can be accounted for. Reach out to me and let me know how it's going. I love to hear from you, and I am always happy to give feedback regularly on my Facebook and Twitter accounts. So without further ado, let's begin, at the beginning.

Parent Engagement 101   1

The future belongs to those who see possibilities before they become obvious.

—John Scully

The concept of parent engagement is not a new one, but that doesn't mean that everyone knows everything there is to know. The reality is, most undergraduate education programs spend very little time focused on teaching incoming educators how to encourage families to engage in the academic world. Yes, most do agree that active parents help students be more successful, but how to get the less active parents to become more active still alludes many. Furthermore, with the additional focus on data and outcomes that come from federal and local legislation and school reform, there has been increasing attention on which variables in the educational world can best be "manipulated" effectively to have the greatest impact on students. It is my opinion that parent engagement is one of the most underserved areas of student support services.

I am often asked, as a so-called expert, what is my definition of parent engagement. Let me go on record as saying, in general, I hate that question. Mainly because it assumes that there is one all-inclusive definition that can be used to judge all schools that either receive the stamp of engagement or do not. In reality, engagement is like life; it's a practice. As the school's population changes or the community evolves, a school can go from having a strong parent presence to struggling. However, if I had to sum it up, I would describe parent engagement as a comprehensive system of connection between families and educational institutions that creates an effective environment for learning. S. Kwesi Rollins, the director of leadership programs at the Washington-based Institute for Educational Leadership, described the two categories of successful engagement practices as "consistent activities that build trust between educators and parents/families; and activities linked to learning that boost the capacity of parents/families to both understand and support their children's learning goals and expectations" (as cited in Rubin, 2015, para. 11). Using this as a springboard, we can acknowledge that engagement must be addressed and assessed in a multifaceted approach.

> Parent engagement is a comprehensive system of connection between families and educational institutions that creates an effective environment for learning.

Looking at the educational system, there are very polarizing views of what "good" parent engagement looks like. People don't always agree on how it is created, monitored, or enhanced. In one setting, parents who check e-mail once a week and donate to the school fundraiser might be seen as engaged. In another setting, parents may feel that they are disinterested if they are not in the building once a week. Though differences in opinion are not uncommon, let's take a brief walk down memory lane with respect to the legislative history of parent engagement to get a general idea of the expectations as our federal government sees them.

Beginning in 1965 with the passage of the Elementary and Secondary Education Act, we were given the Title I portion of the bill (U.S. Department of Education, 2004). This bill addressed the need for improvement in academic achievement of the "disadvantaged," and parent *involvement* became a topic for discussion. The language of the act specified requirements for schools in regard to what interventions they were to introduce for students from low-income families. The exact goal for parent involvement comes from Section 1001, which requires schools to "afford parents substantial and meaningful opportunities to participate in the education of their children" (U.S. Department of Education, 2004, sec. 1001, para. 12). Let the vagueness of that sink in for a moment. The school only really needs to provide an *opportunity* to participate. There is no mention about quantifying "substantial and meaningful," no details about what participation looks like, and, what most educators will quickly note, providing opportunities for participation has very little to do with actually *getting* parents to participate.

In 2001, with the passage of the No Child Left Behind Act, the mandate for engagement was expanded to include any schools who were failing to make adequate yearly progress, regardless of the financial resources of the student body (U.S. Department of Education, 2002). Requirements under this act include a jointly created formalized parent engagement plan, which must be distributed to parents. Federal legislation also provides a penalty for failing to provide proper opportunity and tools to parents.

In the last five years, an increasing number of states have also begun recognizing schools that are more successful at creating "family-friendly" environments. These states, including my home state of Indiana, have created programs that recognize the best and the brightest rather than holding schools accountable for not meeting the standard. Although funding is not necessarily linked to the classification, schools can gain valuable data through the process and ultimately should be able to expect better outcomes.

These state-sponsored initiatives seem to be directly in-line with federal opinion, given the passage of the Every Student Succeeds Act of 2015, which essentially replaces No Child Left Behind. The focus on parent and family engagement is still a primary area for schools to devote attention when seeking to promote the educational advancement of all students. Many of the constructs, with regard to parent and family engagement, are consistent with No Child Left Behind; however, with terms such as "meaningful" and "evidence-based," there is particular attention to incorporating parents as key stakeholders and tracking data linked to engagement.

ENGAGEMENT/INVOLVEMENT/PARTICIPATION

I don't remember when I decided parent engagement was my thing. Going back as far as I can remember, from my time working alongside my parents, serving breakfast, lunch, and sometimes dinner to hungry children in our church, all the way to my first days as a school counselor, I knew that empowered parents make things better for their children and teachers. But when I began looking for information, I found that the research and practice of these topics sometimes leaves too much up for interpretation. For instance, when researching parent "engagement," you will find that the language can be confusing in and of itself. Although the most customary term to be used now is engagement, many educators still use the term "involvement."

I like to be clear and use language that gives life to what I am trying to express. Looking at the *Merriam-Webster Collegiate Dictionary*, we find a definition of engagement that is "emotional involvement or commitment." Involvement, on the other hand, is the "condition of being involved or participating in something" (Engagement, 2015). I liken that difference to a romantic relationship. If one is simply involved, the connotation is casual. However, the idea of an engagement is more formal or consistent.

In her book *Everyday Engagement*, Katy Ridnouer described the process of engaging students as the moment when they are "involved in activities that spark a desire in them" (Ridnouer, 2011, p. 11). My definition of authentically engaging families involves a similar view. Beyond expecting parents to just participate in school-sponsored activities, the goal is to move toward a shared passion for supporting children. I like to say if we are doing it well, parents will feel **competent**, **compelled**, and **committed** to supporting the emotional, academic, and physical development of their children. Table 1.1 shows a chart with examples of how you can comparatively view traditional levels of parent activities to determine the level of engagement.

This is often in stark contrast to what traditional schools define as engagement. Michael Lawson, professor, researcher, and advocate for strong parent involvement in school reform, notes that most schools hold a "school centric" definition of engagement, which basically asks the question, "How can parents support schools and teachers?" (Lawson, 2003). This is likely based on the research that supports the significant positive impact school-focused activities can have on student outcomes, which is strong. Statistically speaking, regardless of socioeconomic, racial, or ethnic background, when parents engage in activities that support the school, children do better (Lawson & Alameda-Lawson, 2012).

Unfortunately, many schools are finding it increasingly difficult to keep substantial attendance at events, beyond a consistent core group of parents. Often, this group has the resources and tools that would likely

Table 1.1 Participation/Involvement/Engagement Comparison

Participation	Involvement	Engagement
Parents regularly attend events	Parents plan events	Parents and staff use pertinent data to decide on interventions and events
Parents receive and review teacher communication	Parents share and act upon information with children	Parents have two-way communication with schools, advocating for needs and receiving responses
Parents volunteer in school activities when requested	Parent volunteers regularly seek opportunities to donate time, services, or goods	Parent volunteers feel connected to school and equally partnered with staff
Parents receive notice of school decisions	Parents receive notice of meetings to discuss decisions	Parents are regularly included in all levels of decision making, from discovery to implementation

lead to them being successful either way. When trying to reach families who are less frequent attendees, schools struggle, finding that there are many barriers to successful implementation. When parents are drawn to attend, the transfer of information is not as seamless as one would hope. Parents may not get what they need, or schools may struggle to present tools and strategies in a clear and concise manner and parents may feel less equipped to use the information that they do receive.

I'll give the example of a recent back-to-school ice cream social I attended. You know the type. Teachers have been frantically prepping classrooms and professionally developing for weeks; they are tired, eager, anxious, and overwhelmed, and at 6 p.m. they are to put on happy faces and greet whoever walks into the room hoping to ease those first-day jitters. Parents rush from work to pick up kids, find parking spaces, stand in line waiting for the doors to be opened, sign in at the front door, and check "the list," which tells the kids which class they will be in for the year. If you, like myself, have more than one child, you try and remember all the names and make your way from room to room to be met with supply lists, get-to-know-me activities, and student info cards. When it's all said and done, you meet in the cafeteria for an ice cream sandwich before you rush home to complete dinner or whatever other activities you have for the evening. Sound familiar?

Before you reach me on Facebook and share with me your glorious stories of ice cream social success, hear me out. I have no problem at all with these types of events, which

> If we are doing it well, parents will feel competent, compelled, and committed to supporting the emotional, academic, and physical development of their children.

we will discuss later in the book, and yes, they absolutely can have a place in your overall parent engagement plan. However, realistically, are these parents *engaged* or simply *involved*? Going back to our working definitions, we could easily say that they are participating and maybe they interact with the teacher enough to qualify for being involved, but it's a far cry from creating lasting emotional commitment. Is it possible to build upon these events and create relationships that are lasting? Sure it is. But that takes consistency and a plan, which unfortunately we may not always have.

A bigger dilemma still is the parents who may never step foot on the school soil or who will only do so when there is a problem: parents who come to sporting events but miss parent teacher conferences, or those who verbalize commitment but lack follow-through. Effectively engaging all families takes into account that the richness of relationship has multiple levels of connection woven together like a beautiful fabric. When we focus on creating this type of relationship, we are more likely to make the type of impact that will lead to sustainable success and less likely to wear ourselves out on ineffective activities.

HISTORICAL DATA ON
PARENT ENGAGEMENT BENEFITS

Building relationships with families is about honoring the hopes and dreams that they have for their children.

—Jackie Garvey

As much as we in education like to believe that politicians sit in an office somewhere passing laws to frustrate and stifle us, as far as parent engagement is concerned, many of the laws with a family engagement focus do have validity. For more than a few decades, we have been able to see substantial research to support the benefit of family engagement in schools. Teachers in schools with high engagement are 50 percent more likely to rate themselves as satisfied with their jobs compared to schools with low family engagement (MetLife Foundation, 2013). The research has been a great help in determining what does and does not work in terms of engagement practices and how they work to ultimately support student achievement. Most of the research has led to categories that are designed to give direction to those seeking to improve parent engagement. One of the most popular names you will hear in the work is Dr. Joyce Epstein. Her work on

| Figure 1.1 | Epstein's Framework Figure |

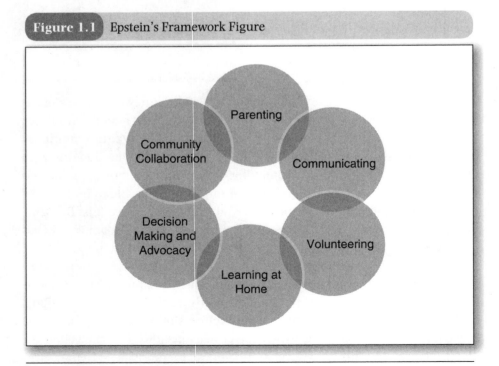

Source: Adapted from Epstein, 2010, Figure 1.2.

the framework of engagement discusses six types of "involvement" necessary to create a foundation of connected parents. In Figure 1.1, you will see a visual representation of these categories.

The biggest takeaway from looking at this framework is that parents must be involved in multiple ways to be successfully engaged. One of the major challenges that many traditional schools face is that they focus on only one or two of these areas of involvement and do not intentionally include all areas systemically in the school functioning levels. Throughout this book, you will be challenged to explore, on multiple levels, all of the ways in which we can effectively engage families long term.

According to evidence by Henderson and Map as published in *Home, School and Community Collaboration: Culturally Responsive Family Engagement*, some of the benefits of strong family engagement include the following:

- Higher grades and test scores
- More accurate academic diagnoses where applicable
- Improved attendance
- Improved social skills
- Reduced behavioral referrals
- Higher graduation rates

Families may also report improved satisfaction with education and increased confidence as parents feel more capable to support their children academically. The benefits for educators have been researched as well. These include teachers feeling more supported and safer in the classroom (Grant & Ray, 2015).

Epstein's model is not the only version currently available. The National Parent Teacher Association (National PTA) model cites six components for strong family partnerships. These components include the following:

- Being welcoming to all families
- Communicating effectively
- Reporting student success
- Including the needs of all children
- Shared power
- Collaboration with the community

The National PTA model includes research on schools with strong parent-teacher organizations; however, in schools with limited or strained parent-teacher relationships, these criteria may be harder to achieve. But remember we're working for progress, not perfection (National PTA, 2015).

For example, one of the schools that I work with is extremely successful in collaborating with the community. Enlace Academy, being a K–fifth-
grade building with a population that is approximately 70 percent native
Spanish speaking, has a particularly challenging job of connecting with
families. While many in the building do speak at least some Spanish, I and
other staff members do not, which poses an interesting dilemma, as you
can imagine. During the first year of the school, it was identified that the
needs of the families in and out of the school were greater than originally
anticipated. By year two of the school's existence, the school added a part-
time social worker, me, to assist families with access to community
resources. The next step was creating partnerships with local agencies
with similar missions of family support. Thus began the process of
expanding school services to share building space with this community
organization. One of the organizations, LaPlaza, partnered to offer a summer camp that was available to both current Enlace families and the community at large. Obviously, these efforts were significant in improving
parents' connections to the school community; however, there were challenges in other areas like developing parent leaders and supporting parents with parenting at home. The attention to building this relationship
was critical in addressing a need for the families and a great place to begin,
but without targeting attention to the other areas like inviting parents to
be decision makers or advocates leaves a gap that still needs to be filled.

Another framework is the Hoover Dempsey and Sandler Model of
Parent Involvement, which was adapted by Ron Mirr in 2009 to address
more of the "messages" that parents can deliver, in various formats, to
encourage school achievement (Mirr, 2009). This model includes similar
categories as the Epstein framework but goes a little further to break down
perceptions and motivations that are needed to support the framework
and how it ultimately connects to the success of individual students.
Beginning strategies address behaviors we hope to see in parents, with
attention given to the influence of parents. There is less attention given to
specific activities that parents can engage in related to the school building
and process and more focus on a pro-education atmosphere that is fos-
tered by parents. Another important idea that this model addresses more
thoroughly is the attention given to the goals of improvement, which
shows that over time, parents lean into attitudes and perceptions of their
children, increasing their own self-efficacy.

What all of these models have in common is that they include more
than one facet of connection. Engagement is about relationship. Like any
relationship, there are multiple dynamics that must be addressed. Would
you want a friend who never listens to you but always tells you to listen to
them? Would you want a family member who wants you to be at all of

their events but never makes it to yours? Would you want a work colleague who is talented but never shares their techniques for achievement with you? Of course not. One-sided, one-dimensional relationships do not build partnerships. Keep this point in mind as you read on.

CURRENT TRENDS IN PARENT ENGAGEMENT

Much of the current research that is used to direct parent and family engagement programs came into focus during the early 2000s and was based on data of that time. However, the drastic changes in the economy and social climate that have taken place in the last ten years have caused some shifts that impact what educators are faced with when they enter the classroom. Because of this, I have included some information on current data with relation to parent and teacher perceptions and behaviors. The newness of this information means that it is more current, but also that there has not been as much time to test implementation theories derived from this data. As we go through the current trends section, understand that the previously noted research still has validity. These new findings can be added to current practices as a method of enhancing program goals and outcomes.

One exciting piece of research that begins to broaden the definition of family engagement is that conducted in 2008 by Yun Mo and Kusum Singh. This research describes three distinct constructs of parents' relationships and involvement in their children's lives:

- Parents' direct involvement in school
- The parent-child relationship
- Parental educational aspirations for the child (Mo & Singh, 2008)

These data are beneficial because they give more direction to where schools can put their energy while investing in improving engagement. These constructs take the perception of parent and family engagement beyond the traditional volunteer model that we see most often. The concept that parents can be engaged solely in relationships with their children or in encouraging expectations without necessarily entering the school building has long been discredited.

In their research, Mo and Singh look at how these different constructs impact the outcomes for students. By polling students about their parents' involvement in areas such as how often their parents asked about school or assisted with school projects, they were able to correlate the findings with the students' performance in school. The research was clear.

Significant impact can be seen, even in the upper elementary and middle school grades, when parents show interest in and support academic interests. The report also gives suggestions for how to create partnerships between school and home, stating, "Schools and parents can create formal and informal ways to have positive and ongoing two-way flow of information and care to support higher school engagement and achievement of young adolescents" (Mo & Singh, 2008, p. 9).

Additional data taken from a small study done by Michael Lawson in 2003 give some background on why these findings are important. The perceptions of parents and teachers are quite divergent. These perceptions lead to some of the inconsistencies in effective parent engagement programs. Parents and teachers from a Title I school with over 800 students and 60 staff were polled in interview and focus group fashion to determine the perceptions that impact the engagement of parents in the building (Lawson, 2003). Some key findings from this study:

- Parents have knowledge of expected involvement in schools.
- Parents have deeper core concerns for their children, which may not connect with these expected activities.
- Parents were reluctant to have honest conversations about schools, on school grounds, alluding to fear.
- Parents' desire for academic success was outweighed, for some, by concerns for basic living needs and survival.
- Parents valued the school commitment to teaching more than academics.
- Some parents felt ignored when it came to the needs of their children.

These and other assertions lead to the necessity of relationships. Parents have a longing for deeper relationships with schools that are focused on holistic development. There is trepidation, especially amongst needy families, as they know the stakes are high. Without an education, the likelihood that their children will be able to achieve or even survive the modern world is unlikely. Parents know this and want a partner in preventing it from coming to pass.

Teachers, however, shared different opinions. Some of the findings of this study echo the sentiments that I shared when describing my parents. Here are some points of note:

- Parents should be there when teachers need them.
- Parents should volunteer regularly in the building.
- Schools need the support of parents through modeling of socially acceptable behaviors.

- Teachers view some parents as deserving of two-way support and others as not, based upon their personal circumstances, such as working hours.
- Teachers view common practices of serving food or offering incentives to parents as "bribery."
- Teachers feel ill-equipped for and overwhelmed by the level of need.

For teachers, most of what they hoped to see in terms of parent engagement can be broken down into two categories: in-school or out-of-school support of school policy, procedures, and activities. Furthermore, the teachers typically acknowledged the needs of the families but felt untrained and experienced varying levels of commitment to addressing these high-level needs.

Some of the general themes were overlapping. For instance, parents' desire for academic success being outweighed by basic living needs was also felt by teachers. The question that is raised is how can schools assist with these needs with shrinking budgets and limited resources, while still trying to overcome academic deficits? In the next chapter, we will look at various family types and begin to brainstorm how to address some of the needs in a thoughtful way.

Vision

- What historical data most surprise you? Why?
- Do you believe the current data about families reflect your building? Why or why not?
- Does your school have an official parent engagement plan?
- If so, what is your role? How effective are you at engaging families?
- As a unit, do you feel you are serving the best interest of the parents and families in your school? Consider 3–5 words you would like to be synonymous with the family engagement efforts of your school or classroom.
- Are you meeting your own expectation?

Plan

- How much time do you plan to devote specifically to parent and family engagement?
- How will you adjust your other duties to make room for this in your day?
- Where, or how, will you document your efforts?

(Continued)

(Continued)

Action

- What is the first step you need to take to move toward a more engaging atmosphere?
- When will you have this step completed?

Notes/Brainstorming

Understanding Parents 2

Any fool can know. The point is to understand.

—Albert Einstein

In the previous chapter, we discussed some of the historical and current research on parent engagement practices. Much of the data previously noted in literature were based on traditional public or private schools with traditional family structures. As we have discovered in practice, some of these techniques are less effective in inner-city, high-needs, public charter, magnet, or low-income or rural schools. In essence, different families have different needs. Professional educators seeking to engage all families need a toolbox that includes a variety of strategies. In this chapter, we will seek to understand the true identity of parents in your buildings. This awareness will be essential in creating an effective plan.

FAMILY STRUCTURES AND PARENT TYPES

I want to make it clear why we are discussing parent "types" in this chapter. In my work with schools, I find it essential that individuals consider the wants, needs, and feelings of the parents who they are trying to engage. It can be hard to discuss these parents anonymously without classifying them in some way. The goal of this chapter is to begin the classification process in an effort to be more responsive to *all* parents. The headings chosen in no way represent all parents' unique characteristics, nor are they given to promote the assumption that parents can only be categorized in one way or all have the same needs. The goal is that these headings are representative of global identifying factors that can be used when determining if your programming is as responsive to all families as it is hoped to be.

Attention has also been given to using people-first language whenever possible to avoid a deficit model of descriptors. However, be aware that these may or may not be labels that parents would appreciate having assigned to them, so whenever speaking directly to specific families, it is advised that you be more suggestive of solutions rather than directive in assigning particular designations to families. Throughout the chapters, there will be references to ideas that may be particularly more effective with certain parent demographics than others; these are again suggestions to assist you with brainstorming and planning from a solution-focused approach. First, we'll look at the overall concept of culture, then we'll discuss various categories that may be present in your school.

WHAT IS CULTURE?

The term culture is such a wonderfully overused and sparsely understood word. Culture is, simply put, a set of values, norms, and behaviors that are shared, typically in an unspoken manner, by a group of people. Most of us define or classify culture by race, religion, or socioeconomic criteria. But in all honesty, culture is really about the lenses through which we look that impact the perceptions and choices that we make. It is important to note that although there are some generally accepted norms among members of a culture, there is no exclusivity on beliefs. This means that within a particular culture there will be differences among individuals that must also be respected and understood.

In a recent conversation with a 16-year-old African American female, she described her frustration with the Black Lives Matter movement. This young lady held hopes of going into law enforcement as a method of providing true justice for all. A noble cause. She often felt misunderstood, and judged, by her fellow students because, as an African American, the expectation was that she would certainly believe in the movement. The assumptions that were placed upon her were incredibly frustrating. She was clear that she wanted the right to make her own judgments and did not want to have people assume that, based upon her culture, she would automatically hold certain beliefs. I tell this story to say this: As we dive into culture, it is important to use this as a guide for planning and preparation and not as a litmus test or scorecard.

The challenge in diversity awareness and cultural sensitivity is that understanding culture can be undermined both by acknowledging our own beliefs and seeking to normalize, as the human brain is created to do. When I began doing home-based therapy, I had to add cultural considerations to all of my comprehensive mental health assessments. This means that I had to consider the cultural norms of each of my clients and how that culture could specifically impact the work that I was going to do with them. Imagine if you had to assume cultural considerations for each student in your care or each member of each family with whom you interact. Cultural considerations can be as simple as assuring that multiple cultures are regularly represented in your classroom or office or as varied as assuring that you invite multicultural speakers to your events. At either end of the spectrum, being aware is the first step to being sensitive, which leads to being competent.

In Figure 2.1, we see an iceberg, which represents the visual and less visual components of culture. It reminds me of my first meeting with a particular client, when I asked her about the relationship that was the basis for our session. During the session, I asked her to tell me about her family. She described her two young children. I went on to probe a little further about her current relationship with her children's father, asking her about how they met and how the relationship progressed. She stopped me and said, "Well, I'm Hispanic."

I asked how this fact applied to our conversation. She went on to say, "In my culture, you have to stay with your baby's father." What she meant was because she had gotten pregnant, her family expected her to develop a relationship and stay with the father of her children. To her this was a norm. No questions asked, clearly understood, common sense, even factual. I was completely unaware of this. Now, I could go out and assume that all Hispanic families will believe the same norms that she does, hoping to have a level of cultural sensitivity. However, I would likely be incorrect and could also offend others in the process of assuming. Cultural competence acknowledges the sameness and uniqueness of any individual within a culture.

Look at Figure 2.1 again. Now let's begin taking it apart to consider with which pieces of the cultural iceberg you are most comfortable. Which areas do you struggle to accept? Which ones are most closely related to your own culture? Do you find this to be accurate or are there other categories you've found?

I was recently listening to a training session that was discussing the impact of chronic absenteeism, and they said one of the ways in which they have been able to make gains is by taking into consideration the way culture can impact attendance. In areas where there are certain religious practices, rather than counting children absent on those days, they have scheduled school breaks more in-line with those times. How

Figure 2.1 Cultural Iceberg

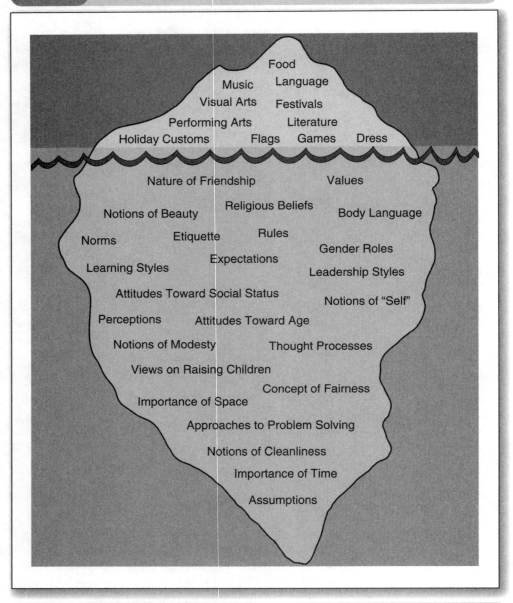

Source: Adapted from http://interculturalism.blogspot.ca/2011/03/iceberg-model-of-culture.html.

responsive is that? When you hear those needs from parents and can, within reason, make adjustments that strengthen partnerships, that is a win for everyone.

It is important to note that the overall concept of parent engagement has a weakness by design. Just as there are no two students alike, there are no two families alike and, therefore, no two parents alike. While parents and families can be categorized, tailoring the parent engagement program to meet the individual needs of parents is one of the most overlooked aspects of authentically engaging families.

> Understanding culture is about a frame of reference to be used as a guide, not a litmus test to define.

Part of a good parent and family engagement program is taking into account the variety of parents and families that make up your school. Categories and labels are less important than understanding the needs of your families. But for the purpose of this book, we will describe those categories and labels so you can understand how the different needs could impact your program. The goal is that you begin to use a lens of engagement that allows you to consider all of the different families as often as possible. Although you won't be able to engage all families all of the time, you will be able to engage more families more often.

Some parenting experts define parents by the way they interact with and/or discipline their children. You may hear terms like "authoritarian" or "free range," "strict" or "lenient," but in terms of the classifications that matter for consideration of parent engagement, we will discuss the differences in parents that can sometimes make it more complicated when planning events or activities. Keep in mind, many families will fit into multiple categories.

WORKING PARENTS

Approximately 60 percent of families with children have two parents working outside of the home, according to 2014 United States Department of Labor statistics (U.S. Department of Labor, Bureau of Labor Statistics, 2015). This has a tremendous impact on the amount of time that parents may have available to participate in events, help with homework, or actively engage in school-sponsored activities. You will find many parents in less affluent areas who may even be working multiple jobs, which makes free times nearly nonexistent. The thoughts, feelings, and needs of working parents can range from being career focused and driven to being overwhelmed and overworked.

SINGLE PARENTS

While still the minority, the most recent information from the Kids Count Data Center shows that approximately 35 percent of students are currently living in single-parent households (Kids Count Data Center, 2015). From parents who have chosen to adopt or give birth without a partner to those who are single due to death or divorce, as educators we must acknowledge that, consistently, one-third of students are being primarily raised by one parent.

Like all parents, single parents are capable of providing a loving and supportive environment for their children to thrive; however, the needs of single parents may be different at times than those of two-parent households. I've worked in several schools that had large single-parent populations. In some instances, the mother or father had a strong support system and managed well; in others, the parent felt ill-equipped for the task and needed a great deal of support. The idea is to consider that a single parent may have additional challenges or needs and look for ways to offset that. When I was a middle school counselor, we planned a mother-and-daughter event, and we assumed that some of our mothers would be working; we also assumed that some would be unable to attend because they needed to stay home with other siblings. When we created the invitations, instead of saying "mother and daughter" we said "student and woman of importance." Some girls brought an older sibling or aunt and others were with parents. For girls who did not have a mother figure available, we also had volunteer moms from the community available. Removing barriers is a critical way to increase connection.

ENGAGING FATHERS

Engaging fathers begins with educating them on their value to our children. Many men still view their worth in terms of monetary contribution. Factors such as their own relationship with their fathers, their confidence in their abilities, and the extenuating obligations that they have also contribute to the amount of effort they may be willing to exhibit toward the education of their children. For example, a father may see the importance of teaching his children to perform household maintenance tasks but not see the value of things like homework or extra-curricular clubs. It is important for schools to build upon the strengths of fathers and leverage those into benefits for all students.

It is also worth noting that there seems to be some difference in the level of engagement as it relates to relationship status. In *What Successful Schools Do to Involve Families*, several studies were cited that pointed to the importance of engaging both single fathers as well as fathers in committed relationships (Glasgow & Whitney, 2009). The research suggests that fathers who are in relationships tend to be less involved than single fathers. While there may be multiple reasons, I would hypothesize that some fathers feel more inclined to be active if there is no mother in the picture to assist or if there is a strong desire to maintain a connection outside of the marital relationship.

Most schools would say that engaging any father is a challenge, but some have been extremely successful. The following are a few ideas that I have seen be effective.

Father and Child Events. My husband is a father of four daughters, and over the course of 22 years he has attended numerous father-and-daughter breakfasts, lunches, or dinners. He loves them, goes way overboard in prepping, and has the time of his life. Providing semi-structured activities like this can be really helpful in modeling appropriate interactions. Taking some of the pressure off of planning also allows fathers to focus on strong relationships.

Traditionally Male Events. Things like golf outings and sports-themed activities appeal more to fathers who are less interested in making crafts or simply academic events. When possible, connect these events with curriculum or specific content to get the biggest bang for your buck.

Have Fathers Invite Fathers. For some men, having overly zealous volunteer moms invite them to events is off-putting. A casual invitation from a man with a focus on assuring the father that their participation will be enjoyable and meaningful to their children is key. If possible, a personal phone call is great.

Create an Atmosphere That Is Gender Neutral. Because in many schools the majority of staff and volunteers are female, it is easy to overlook some simple details that can be more inclusionary for fathers. Beststart.org provides a resource guide for working with fathers, and they cite the following areas where fathers can be encouraged to feel more comfortable:

- Make sure the space where you have events is not cramped. Fathers may not be comfortable sharing tight spaces.
- Offer magazines and stories with male leads and interests.
- Ensure that there is a male-friendly changing area for dads who need to change their children.

Competition Is a Good Motivator. While moms may be drawn to collaborative events, some dads prefer a healthy game or competition.

Adding competition to themed events can be a big draw. Steer away from participation awards, which most dads shun.

Because of the value of fathers in education, there are several school-based programs that provide training and tools in a ready-to-go format. We will discuss two of those here.

All Pro Dad

Founded over a decade ago as an extension of Family First, this not-for-profit father empowerment group focuses on encouraging fathers through daily e-mails, monthly meetings, and yearly father-and-child events to be strong positive influences in the lives of their children and the community. The no-pressure atmosphere of the meetings is less PTO and more father support, with an air of connecting fathers around a unified goal.

This national organization has the support of major celebrities and professional sports organizations and, though often headed by spiritual leaders, does not discriminate against any religion. The activities are designed to increase the amount of quality time fathers spend with their children, and the regular communication that is shared via e-mail and social media gives snippets of life tips for fathers navigating the modern parenting world (All Pro Dad, 2015).

WATCH D.O.G.S

Founded in 1998, WATCH D.O.G.S. (Dads Of Great Students) was designed as a father engagement program to increase male role models for all children and support the school security and safety by adding additional male presence to the building. Asking for the simple commitment of one day per year, the goal is to get fathers to the building and to let them know that their presence alone does wonders.

Currently in 46 states and abroad, the program has achieved national recognition for its effort to support both the staff and students in the building. Developed under the National Center on Fathering, the goal is obviously to empower fathers, but with training and attention to survey and school data, the impact for schools is undeniable (National Center for Fathering, 2015).

PARENTS LIVING IN POVERTY

Ruby Payne's groundbreaking research on poverty continues to be controversial. Many have spoken against her findings, stating that she focuses almost entirely on the negative impact of poverty and ignores strengths within the individuals who live in impoverished conditions. However, the science behind her research continues to prove what she hypothesized then, which is that poverty has an impact on the development and processing function of the brain. This impact can be seen as "superficially" as the IQ of students living in poverty or as deeply as the neurological functioning of the amygdala. The amygdala is the emotional regulation hub of the brain. The impact of poverty on children is that they struggle to maintain moods and regulate emotion, including emotional expression into adulthood. So when you have parents who are products of generational poverty, they likely are experiencing the challenges of both their own childhood and the impact of trying to provide for their own children. This can make for difficult conversations, miscommunications, and seemingly maladaptive behaviors, which leave educators increasingly frustrated. A 2007 study of administrators in schools with high poverty (defined as those schools with at least 60 percent low-income students) notes that engaging parents and the community is more difficult for them than for those who work in schools with fewer low-income students (MetLife Foundation, 2007).

One of the best and simplest articles that I have ever seen on working with parents in poverty was published on the website Cornerstone for Teachers by Angela Watson. In her article, she discussed the sometimes frustrated, always complicated mind-set that is often shared by parents living in poverty, citing an example of a mother who regularly struggled financially, spending a windfall tax refund on a coat instead of a more responsible use of the funds. Watson notes that she had previously felt empathy for the mother but in this situation found herself almost angry with her choice. She acknowledges blaming the mother for irrational choices and feeling disconnected from her in the process (Watson, 2014).

So how does one move past this anger, which often turns into an adversarial standoff? The first step is to acknowledge the internal frustration. You are not "wrong" for wanting your families to have the best and make the most of their resources. But if you allow that to impact the way you view the parents, offer support or encouragement, or how you interact with them daily, you will be doing yourself and your students a disservice. In this country, we have a very difficult time communicating about polarizing topics. Discussing race, religion, politics, or poverty can quickly turn friends into enemies. Attempting to understand families requires that you understand your own biases and beliefs.

For many teachers, they simply want the why. Science is helping us with that and essentially giving us a

> When working with families living in poverty:
>
> - Start small and work from there
> - Be aware of your own values and potential biases
> - Don't take their choices as an attack on you

way to connect in the process. In her article, Watson referenced the 2013 study that led to the printing of "Poverty Impedes Cognitive Function," which discussed many of the biological differences that we see in the brains of students who live in families with limited financial resources (Watson, 2014). Simply put, living under constrained conditions limits your perspective and processing. The limits can be long term and seem to exist even when financial conditions change. So, for example, parents who are now working or financially middle class who grew up poor may still be processing things differently than your families who have been consistently financially comfortable. Your goal with these families is to begin to broaden the horizon in an achievable way.

There is a school near my home in Indianapolis that markets itself as "college or die." They seek to make college the functional and cultural norm of the school in order to remove some of the stigma or mystery of the post-secondary experience. This is a great concept. However, for some families, it is so far beyond the realm of their reality that they are not even attracted to the school. Knowing what your families' dreams are helps you take them one step past where they are. With each step, there is another chance to move them closer to the ultimate goal of academic, emotional, and social success, but taking them from zero to 60 might be too far, too fast. When you are dealing with families who are struggling with long-term systems of poverty, start small and work your way up. Do not get discouraged by what may seem to you to be illogical thinking, and understand that your own values may be foreign to them and their poor choices are not a personal attack on you.

Beginning with the passage of federal funding for early childhood education, we began to accept the knowledge that in order to help families in poverty, we needed to not only start earlier in getting students ready for school but also help support parents. This multigenerational approach is one that works well for a local preschool program in my area. St. Mary's child care has a rich history in the community as being extremely successful at helping preschool children minimize the gap in learning that typically exists between children living in poverty and their middle-class counterparts.

PARENTS OF STUDENTS WHO RECEIVE SPECIAL EDUCATION SERVICES

Over the course of my career, I have worked with numerous parents at various stages of parenting children with special education needs. A family friend of mine whose son was entering kindergarten after a recent diagnosis of Autism found herself getting a crash course in the

Individuals with Disabilities Education Act (IDEA), the Americans with Disabilities Act of 1990 (ADA), and the Individualized Education Plan (IEP). Our conversations were brief, but she took them and put them to work for her with all of the passion she could muster and got great results as she partnered with her child's school and her medical care providers.

However, it is not at all uncommon for special education-certified educators to feel unsupported by parents who do not seem to understand the needs of their children or how hard they, being the educator, work to provide equal access to education for each student. This can lead to disconnection and the potential for misunderstanding both ways.

In many ways, working with parents of special education students is in no way different than any other parents; in other ways, it can be a completely unique experience. But according to the MetLife survey of 2012, engaging parents of diverse learners, particularly those impacted by poverty, continues to be a challenge to school leaders as they note both feeling unprepared and having limited success (MetLife Foundation, 2013).

Some items to consider when working with parents of special education students include, but are not limited to, the following:

- *Language.* The world of special education has enough acronyms to make a pot of alphabet soup. New parents may not understand any of what you are talking about. Be clear, check for understanding often, and do not assume silence equals understanding.
- *Emotional responses.* As my opening anecdote described, the process that parents go through as they process the diagnoses that their children are being given can elicit a variety of responses. From grief to relief, parents are checking and adjusting the dreams that they have for their children right in the moment, and this must be handled with compassion and empathy. Validation is key.
- *Conflict.* There is no greater source of conflict between a parent and educator than when the parent feels the needs of their child are not being met. With parents of special education students, the level of needs of the children may mean that the parents become more vigilant and committed to excellence for their child. This can pose conflicts when the school has an alternative opinion. Expecting the potential for conflict is reasonable. Managing and resolving conflicts is a skill that takes patience and practice.

PARENTS WITH LIMITED ENGLISH LANGUAGE

It is not uncommon for educators to be challenged in working with families who are English language learners. While most have good intentions, everything from language barriers to unknown cultural expectations can impact the connection and communication. Parents who may not even understand a word you are saying are trusting you with their child. And you as an educator are expecting to impart knowledge using resources that may have never been designed to teach them. There is a common ground in the idea that you are both going for the same goal. Building upon that helps strengthen the relationship.

In her book *Involving Latino Families in Schools: Raising Student Achievement Through Home School Partnerships*, Dr. Concha Delgado Gaitan speaks about the commonalities that teachers have with families (Delgado Gaitan, 2004). Some of the ones she listed include the following:

- Shared value in education
- High expectations for their children
- Parents respect school leaders' authority

While her research was specifically based on Latino families, similar values can be seen in other demographics as well. These acknowledgments are important because they serve as the basis for connections when language, traditions, and lifestyle may differ significantly.

Working in a school with 70 percent English language learners has taught me quite a bit about working with families where English is not the first language. Whether these families are new to the United States or have been here for several years, traditionally, families of English language learners have a higher commitment to the family unit. Engaging these families works well when including all members of the family regardless of age.

Each year at Enlace we host an international festival. This serves as an opportunity for all families to share cultural expressions through food, music, dance, or art. Staff also participates, sharing their cultural experiences. A deeper level of connecting and understanding when families come from a variety of backgrounds requires a climate of cultural inclusion where students are welcomed and encouraged to include their own heritage in every aspect of the academic setting. This should be shared with family as well.

YOUNG PARENTS

In 1970, the average age of a first-time parent was 21. By 2006, that number had increased to 25 (Livingston & Cohn, 2010). While that number is not alarmingly different, the truth behind that number is that many adults are waiting longer to begin having children. Data from the National Center for Health Statistics and the Census Bureau were combined to reveal some interesting trends that the Pew Research Center used in the report "The New Demographic of American Motherhood." Notes of interest include the number of teen parents decreasing and the number of births in women age 35 and older increasing (Livingston & Cohn, 2010). These numbers are due in part to improvements in fertility treatment and more professional women delaying childbirth in favor of focusing on careers. Because of these trends, parents of elementary students who are younger than 30 or parents of secondary students who are under 40 may be a rarity in some suburban districts.

With more parents being older, connecting with younger parents is an area to consider. One aspect of culture is age. Pop culture website Toottoot. com lists several common facts about people who were born in 1980:

- They have never known the world without AIDS.
- They have always had cable.
- The Internet has always existed for them.
- Popcorn has always been cooked in a microwave.

Now while this little walk down memory lane may make some of us feel old, the reality is when we communicate with people who have a different frame of reference than us, we have to be careful to make sure that we are consciously engaging them and not being condescending. I can recall being a young kindergarten parent and the feeling of being spoken to as if I were a child rather than the adult responsible for caring for my child. Since educators are typically seen in an authoritative light, we want to include some attention to intentionally avoiding a superior placement over all parents, but specifically over young parents.

PARENTS OF AT-RISK OR CHALLENGING KIDS

This section is particularly special to me as a self-proclaimed advocate for students who are at risk. In my book *Drag 'Em Kicking and Screaming: Your Seven-Step Action Plan for At-Risk Student Success*, my co-authors and I outlined 34 tips designed to help educators build meaningful relationships with students. These relationships then became the foundation for leading children to personal success. In some segments of the educational community, the term "at-risk" has become a derogatory term, giving the connotation that the students lack skills necessary to be successful. My use of the term speaks solely to the research given on how certain demographic characteristics, readily documented in detail for multiple years by the U.S. Department of Education, have been shown to place students at a greater likelihood of failing to make adequate yearly progress, graduate high school, or successfully transition to post-secondary educational opportunities. The term is not used to propose that these students are in any way less capable or valuable.

I do think it is worth noting that not all educators share my zest for working with at-risk students. With additional pressures being placed on educator effectiveness by oversized classrooms, limited resources, and sometimes skills that are years behind their peers, it is reasonable to see why there would be frustration.

Working with at-risk students is one of my specialties. Charlie Applestein calls them "tough" kids, but, truth be told, I really enjoy working with the hard cases. Kids who are just this side of failure speak to me because these are the kids who have likely been hurt or have the greatest need. They often long for connection and attachment and will ask for both in the most unloving ways. The tough part of this scenario is that without parents, the long-term prognosis for these kids is not great. Even with the parents on board, the odds are not in their favor, but empowering parents is one of the best chances that they have. Teachers agree with this. In 2008, nearly two-thirds of teachers in urban school districts noted that low parent engagement was a contributing factor to at least a quarter of their students underperforming (MetLife Foundation, 2007).

Connecting with parents of at-risk kids can be incredibly difficult. This is due in part to the idea that parents may be to blame for at least some of what has caused the student to be in this position. It is important to note that many parents of at-risk kids were at-risk kids themselves. Many of them had challenging experiences in education or life and have their own needs to address. The systemic and generational root causes of these ongoing factors absolutely impact the parents' impressions of the school setting. Therefore, getting parents to connect with the school can require some intentional efforts on the part of educators. Convincing them that they can help their children learn may seem like an insurmountable task, but once they commit, these can be some of your greatest allies.

In her book *Help for Billy*, Heather Forbes describes some tips for engaging families with kids whose behaviors are challenging. She suggests brief communications to summarize daily school events and nightly home events (Forbes, 2012). In my school, many teachers do this via text. Some even use a "positive text home" as a positive behavior intervention. Forbes also recommends directly and personally connecting with parents and utilizing strategies that work well in both settings. This may mean that parents use techniques from the classroom and also that teachers will be willing to use strategies from home.

Many times, the behavior we see in challenging or at-risk kids is actually related to traumatic events. This trauma may have occurred because of the parents, but there are many instances when the parents, too, were victims. Considering this helps temper the often strained and stressful relationship that develops between parents and staff when kids are "difficult."

OLDER PARENTS

Growing up, I thought my parents were old. No kidding. Having me in their early 40s was a choice and one that they often speak of as being a good one, but in the 1980s, having parents nearing 50 while in elementary school was uncommon. Now, the term "older parent" has changed. With many more parents waiting until after they have successfully begun a career or who have struggled with fertility issues, delayed parenthood is no longer an anomaly. The term "older" in terms of parenting can be beyond age 40 and may include grandparents who are raising their children's children or family members who never had children raising extended family or fostering youth.

The age difference can be challenging on both ends, with older adults feeling lost in a world with which they are unfamiliar and younger teachers feeling uncomfortable being in the role of leadership with people who are older than themselves. The best tip I have for this population is to assume nothing, inquire always, and explain when necessary. I know some 50-somethings who are better on Facebook than my 16-year-old and others who are still afraid of it. Simply asking, "Are you familiar with our Facebook page?" is both unassuming and at the same time informative. If you have a large population of parents who you think could benefit from assistance and not enough time to ask everyone individually, send out an FYI-type newsletter to give everyone the same content. Most parents who do not need it will not be offended, and those who do will be very grateful.

PARENTS OF STUDENTS IN AN ALTERNATIVE EDUCATION SETTING

My number one tip for working with parents while being in an alternative setting is to understand that these are parents who have most likely been through a fair amount of disappointment. Whether their child has been sent to the alternative setting because of their academics or behavior, it's likely that these parents never planned for this to occur. They have probably taken off of work more times than they care to mention, may have even lost jobs due to missed days. They may have families who blame them or have all but written them off.

It is possible that you may find these parents are mentally or physically exhausted. Remember, it is unlikely that these children are unruly with you and angels when they get home. While your instinct may be to blame the parents due to your exhaustion level, it may only be a mild representation of what they are experiencing with their child at home. Sometimes in addition to the school issues, as early as elementary school, children begin receiving criminal charges for their behavior, making parents have school and court to contend with, including court-ordered services, restitution, and the ever-watchful eye of the juvenile justice center.

In other instances, the parents may be a major contributing factor to the child's admittance into the alternative program. Perhaps there is a mental health or addiction issue that has caused the parent to be inactive or less effective in parenting. Parents may be actively engaged in their own struggle or criminal activity and have little time, energy, or willingness to participate in services. It is even possible that the trauma the child may have experienced was also experienced by the parent.

With all that being said, it is no wonder that connecting with families in an alternative setting will be less about take-home activity packs and more about connecting with families and connecting them to outside resources. For the most part, the needs in an alternative setting will be high, well beyond the scope of what the school can reasonably expect to provide on an ongoing basis. Thinking outside the box is only the tip of the iceberg. Here are a few ideas to get you started.

The first step in connecting with families is collaborating with your community. Offer your building, or parking lot, for back-to-school or holiday events, then make sure that your families are aware of the requirements for participation. Aside from sharing space, typically the cost is low and there is shared work versus your school trying to provide all of the needs.

Another option is rather than trying to provide in-house parenting or mentoring services, solicit a local church or several religious institutions and ask for them to provide mentors for your students. Aside from providing opportunity and space for the interactions, there will usually be no cost to the school and the needs will still be met.

EARLY CHILDHOOD LEARNERS

Engaging parents of early childhood learners may, on the surface, seem like an easy task. After all, during this early time in development, parents are still in the mind-set of their children needing extra help, unlike parents of older students who may feel that children need to have more independence and autonomy. We spoke about some of the work done at St. Mary's Children's Center in Indianapolis with regard to their work with children living in poverty. Opened in 1961, their commitment has led to a rich history of working to help preschoolers enter kindergarten on target. You may not realize that for families living in poverty, a population that continues to grow in this country, the average student will enter kindergarten one and a half to two years behind their middle-class counterparts. St. Mary's uses some innovative curriculum strategies to make up for the gap in learning that often is created when parents have to spend more time on survival than on academically enriching their preschoolers. Beyond curriculum, however, the staff at St. Mary's prides

Figure 2.2 Family Showcase

themselves on supporting the whole family, which is a great way of developing the child holistically. Here are some ways that St. Mary's incorporates the parents in their school.

In Figure 2.2, you see a photo of a family showcase. St. Mary's holds several family events during the course of the school year, and during those times the families are assisted with engaging in activities with the children with the guidance of the staff. These events are then turned into a showcase for all to see, highlighting the skills that they taught as well as the enjoyment of the activity. Modeling play as well as academics is an important piece to consider when working with early learners. Acknowledging the whole development of the child from the very beginning lays an amazing foundation for future work.

Another way to incorporate the significance of family time outside of school and allow the students to have simple reminders of family throughout the day is to hang family photos around the student work area. Both of these examples are extensions of regular programming, such as home visits, personal interviews, and direct therapeutic and social services available to the entire family in the wrap-around approach that has been shown to be very effective and closely resembles the collaborative care model.

Regardless of your setting or parent type in your program, the goal of identifying parents is only to gain greater insight in attempting to build relationships with parents. Identifying the types of parents in your building is the first step, but understanding their needs is not only critically important but also an area where many schools drop the ball, so to speak. For example, a school may want to increase the amount of reading in the home so they focus on reading logs and a campaign to promote reading in the home, including positive reinforcement, but the reading does not improve. Why? There are various reasons, but let's say that I do not own any books in my home; would it be possible for me to read? Maybe, if I am aware of libraries or I have the ability to borrow books. As a school, if we focused our attention on the belief that parents did not understand the importance of reading, we would miss the reality that they needed resources for reading. Identifying thoughts, feelings, and needs is the reason I created the parent empathy map. Figure 2.3 is a parent empathy map, which helps you better understand the often unseen perceptions that effect a parent's willingness or ability to engage in school-related activities. Completing the empathy map for a "hard to reach" or "challenging" parent helps you with empathy and brainstorming solutions, both of which are essential for improving relationships.

| Figure 2.3 | Parent Empathy Map |

What do parents think and feel?

What do parents see and hear?

What are parents saying and doing?

What do parents want?

What pains do parents have?

What gains are parents making?

CURRENT RESEARCH ON PARENTS

I am always amazed by educators' perception of parents. The media and even other parents can also be extremely harsh with regard to parents. In 2011, one-third of teachers and nearly 50 percent of parents stated that they felt that parents were not interested enough in their children's education (MetLife Foundation, 2013). I already told you how many educators would have viewed my parents. In fact, I have asked some in my professional development sessions and typically there is a split decision on whether my parents were engaged. Some go as far as saying that my parents must have been engaged since their children, meaning me, seem to be successful; others point out that certain traits are essential and, when lacking, automatically mean there is a deficit in engagement. Whether in my work or in my social circles, people are always quick to chime in with their opinions of the flawed education system. While there is some blame placed on the educators, very often I hear teachers and the general public complaining about "those" parents who do not parent or do not support teachers. The impression I get is that parents don't know what they are doing, or they are too busy trying to be friends with their children and don't want to enforce rules. But you know what, I am a parent. I'm not consumed with being my children's friend and I am committed to supporting educators as they support my children. I am a professional parent coach so I have a great deal of knowledge, yet I don't always know what to do. I'm also under the impression that parents of today love their children just as much as parents of the '60s, '70s, and '80s. If you google how to raise kids, you'll get over 49 million google hits. Proof that parenting is hard!

It is not at all uncommon for educators to say they don't know what parents want. Because of that, it can be difficult to determine what to improve; where to invest time, energy, or resources; or what to eliminate from your parent engagement efforts all together. Communicating with parents via parent survey is a great place to begin. However, particularly when engagement is low, it is hard to get solid data. What we could use at this point is some independently achieved information to help us begin the brainstorming process. In 2009, the Equality and Human Rights Commission conducted extensive research on modern parents in Great Britain and their perceptions of parenting and children. Eighty-five percent of parents polled valued their children as the first priority of the family (Ellison, Barker, & Kulasuriya, 2009). Research was conducted in the United States, even more recently, that speaks to the same underlying themes:

- In November 2014, NBC News conducted a survey of parents that yielded some incredible data. Approximately 51 percent of parents currently believe that they are more active in their children's lives than their parents were with them (NBC News Education Nation, 2014).
- Depending on race, between 40 and 60 percent of parents also wish that they could be doing more. This shows that parents are both aware of the value of involvement with their children and consciously attempting to improve what they do beyond what their parents did and even what they have done in the past (NBC News Education Nation, 2014).
- According to a MetLife survey, more than seven in 10 teachers and administrators note engaging parents and the community as important in improving education but also note that it is either challenging or very challenging to accomplish (MetLife Foundation, 2013).

These data create a clear impression that parents are not as uninvolved as we may believe, and, more importantly, there is at least some desire to be more involved. Contrary to popular belief, the concept that parents are disinterested or even apathetic, as we may believe from looking at their absence from the school, may be pretty far from the truth. In my opinion, this is a great indication that parental absence does not equal indifference. Keep in mind that parents really do feel that they are doing better, but many still want to improve. Use this in your direction of parents and support of the desired outcome.

A more unfortunate piece of data that came out is that despite current and historical research to the contrary, most parents, **87 percent** in fact, still believe that the outcomes for their children are more determined by the child's ability than the impact that parents can have (NBC News Education Nation, 2014). This point will be important to remember when thinking about special situations, like parents of children with learning disabilities or special education needs. Referring to the empathy map we spoke about earlier in the chapter, if a parent believes that a child's ability level is low, and yes, you will have parents who have resolved themselves to the "fact" that their child is incapable of improving, the likelihood that they will be willing to engage in specific activities to change that belief is lessened. That is a thought you have to combat directly or be ready to address with resources or tools. It's also important with students of average or above-average intelligence or academic abilities. Parents who believe that their children don't need them are also not as likely to be as involved as a school may like. Perhaps there is an enrichment program, but you find parents not willing to let the child attend because they don't truly see the value in the program and believe the child will do fine without it. The goal is to help parents see their value. Our traditional methods of communicating this to parents sometimes fall short of the empowerment that we would hope to see.

The PDK/Gallop Poll of 2015 reveals some data on parents' perceptions related to standardized tests and curriculum, two topics that many educators believe parents don't know enough or care enough about. In this poll, which sampled over 3,000 adults, most agreed again that Common Core does not support the type of learning that they believe to be most important for students. Most adults believe parents have the right to pull their kids from standardized testing, and often these parents also believe that focusing on testing is impacting the ability of schools to teach children necessary skills. The emotional toll of testing is also a concern for most adults. If we can use this information to empower parents to vote and support the legislation that will make a difference for the children, educators would feel less like they are out in the shark-infested waters fighting for kids alone (PDK International, 2015).

All of this research really shows that parents do want their children to do well; they want to be supportive and have a strong desire to make an impact. However, for many schools, tapping into this desire has been hard, if not almost impossible, to do. As we move forward through these chapters, if you find yourself getting stuck in what the parents "don't" do, be very clear that the "don't" does not necessarily equal "won't." Your goal is to tap into the parent desires, needs, and feelings and use those to provide supports for the family. These supports can then create a foundation for the healthy development of your students.

PARENT SURVEY (ASK NOT WHAT YOUR PARENTS CAN DO FOR YOU, ASK WHAT YOU CAN DO FOR YOUR PARENTS)

If you are fortunate enough to have parents who are willing to provide you with specific information, this can be much more helpful than general information. We will review a few sample questions and tools for gathering data here and some of the best practices for acquiring results.

Most of the organizations that allow schools or programs to be recognized for parent engagement require that a survey of parents be completed to give the parent perspective on the efforts of the school. However, outside of this type of review program, many schools rarely ask for this info from parents and those that do usually get it from a select group. Below are a few sample questions you might want on your survey:

- How often do you hear from your child's teacher? Would you like more, less, or the same?
- What is your preferred method of communication regarding your child?
- Do you feel comfortable asking for help from the school?
- What skills do you have that you would like to share with our staff and students?

The questions on the survey can be as specific or general as you need them to be. For example, if you are looking to add programming, you can include specific questions about the program components; however, you might also ask what type of social media parents regularly use. A parent survey allows you to get practical current information as well as long-range goals for future planning. Open dialogue is hugely beneficial for schools when looking to improve engagement. If your school has not conducted a parent survey this year, it may feel daunting to put one together. Figure 2.4 shows a sample survey that can be used to get a general overview of parent interest and needs.

BOILING IT DOWN: WHAT PARENTS WANT

We've looked at broad categories of parent types and perceptions and even discussed some of the ways you can gain valuable data from parents, but translating that into programs that meet the needs of parents as well as the goals of the school can be challenging. It can sometimes feel as if parents and schools are naturally at odds. While currently this may be true, in order to move toward improving outcomes for students, it is essential that there be a team approach.

The good news is that parents generally believe that teachers, and schools, are doing a good job. And when presented with empowering data and tools, parents will very often rise to the challenge of supporting schools and weary educators. In Indiana, where I live, over the past 10 years, school districts have struggled to balance the budget and often looked to creative ways of increasing revenue for local public districts. Creating referendums for strapped school districts was risky for many years, with a 50/50 pass rate once it made it to the ballot. By 2014, this changed considerably, with most districts passing, with reasonable margins, legislation that increased taxes and provided that money to schools

Figure 2.4 Sample Parent Survey

Dear parent or guardian:

Please help us gain more information about how we as a school are doing at supporting you and your child. Please complete the survey and feel free to put any additional comments or concerns on the back of this form.

AREA OF SERVICE	QUALITY RATING					
	Strongly agree	Agree	Neutral	Disagree	Strongly disagree	Don't know
OVERALL IMPRESSIONS						
Our school provides a quality education for your child.	1	2	3	4	5	6
Our school is doing an excellent job teaching:						
Reading	1	2	3	4	5	6
Writing	1	2	3	4	5	6
Math	1	2	3	4	5	6
Science	1	2	3	4	5	6
Physical Education	1	2	3	4	5	6
Fine Arts	1	2	3	4	5	6
I communicate well with my child's teacher.	1	2	3	4	5	6
SCHOOL RESOURCES						
The school provides my child with everything that he or she needs to learn.	1	2	3	4	5	6
The school building is well maintained and appropriate for learning.	1	2	3	4	5	6
LIFE SKILLS TRAINING						
My child receives education on social skills that will help him or her be successful.	1	2	3	4	5	6
The school does a good job preparing my child for the future.	1	2	3	4	5	6
I believe the school does a good job preparing all children for the future.	1	2	3	4	5	6
BEHAVIOR						
I believe the children in the school treat each other respectfully.	1	2	3	4	5	6
I understand the school discipline policies.	1	2	3	4	5	6
Children in our school are culturally sensitive.	1	2	3	4	5	6
Staff at the school are culturally sensitive.	1	2	3	4	5	6
The structure of the school day and activities helps the children learn.	1	2	3	4	5	6
Staff at the school care about my child.	1	2	3	4	5	6
PARENT-SCHOOL COMMUNICATION						
As a parent I feel welcome in the school.	1	2	3	4	5	6
As a parent I feel my opinion is taken seriously at the school.	1	2	3	4	5	6

(McInerny, 2014). Because the public was educated on the benefit for the school, voter turnout increased, and many claimed their primary focus was in voting for a tax increase to help schools. This is the definition of engaged communities and shows that one thing parents and community members support is transparency and honesty. Telling parents you need an extra $50 per house for buses is something most can get behind if they understand for what they are working.

Quite simply, educated parents support educators. The problem is that very often parents aren't sure what they are opposed to or supporting. It is the job of the school to change that. One organization that has done an amazing job of empowering parents to be aware and informed is In*Source Special Education Support. In 1975, a group of parents, passionate about supporting their children with disabilities, came together to assure that their children received the support they were entitled to under the newly enacted IDEA and ADA laws that gave all children access to fair and equitable education in a public school setting. Prior to that time, many of their children had been unable to attend school. Over the years, In*Source has grown to include paid staff, volunteers statewide, training, and conference opportunities for parents and educators, and they have created partnerships which have bettered the lives of countless students. Understand that the majority of these participants are parents; not educators, not legislators, but parents given proper tools who are using them to make a difference for students.

Empowering parents can feel like one more burden on the already full plate of the educator, and that is why organizations like In*Source, which can partner with schools, make the most sense. This falls under the sixth key of Epstein's framework as community collaboration. Schools can donate space and/or time to community organizations like In*Source, making it easier for parents to get the information that they need in one location.

Vision

- What types of parents do you have in your school?
- How successful at engaging each type of parent are you? (Have each team member complete an empathy map for one type of parent, share in a group meeting, and discuss strategies for meeting each of the needs raised.)
- What community organizations can you include in your next event to give parents access to resources and education in one location?

(Continued)

(Continued)

- Have you completed a parent survey or needs assessment?
- What other topics should you include in your parent surveys or needs assessments?

Plan

- Based upon your parent surveys, who else do you need to include in the process?
- When will you make contact with these individuals or groups?
- What funding sources do you have available for this program?

Action

- How often should you conduct the needs assessment and surveys?
- How will they be distributed?
- Do you have a formal team for addressing the data collected?

Notes/Brainstorming

Defining
the Goals

3

The trouble with not having a goal is that you can spend your life running up and down the field and never score.

—Bill Copeland

If you ask 100 educators what engagement means to them, you will likely get 100 different answers.

In fact, I did just that. I asked educators, via confidential survey, how they would describe an engaged parent. Here are some of the direct quotes from these surveys.

"Interested in more than just when their student is in trouble."

"An engaged parent or guardian is someone who is willing to communicate with the teacher and staff. It is someone who recognizes and accepts that the teachers and school staff want what is the absolute best for their child and their peers."

"A parent who knows what is going on in a child's education and supports them in that in whatever capacity they are able."

"An engaged parent is active in their child's education and willing to help in any way."

While we know that descriptions of engagement can vary, in the opinion of these educators some common themes generally come up, from consistent communication to an overall support of quality education for all students. Things like positive communication, enriching home environments, and support of educators in both theory and practice are topics that come up often. In general, educators know and can clearly articulate what they do not want, but clarifying the things that they do want parents to do is sometimes a little cloudier. Knowing what you don't want is a good start, but you can't score if you aren't shooting for a goal.

To challenge educators to get really clear about the engagement that they wanted to see, I used an activity to start the creative juices flowing. In the activity, I described parents by some basic characteristics like demographics, home activities, and perceptions of educators and asked the teachers to rate the family as either engaged or not. Across the board, they were split nearly in half in relation to whether or not they would classify a parent as engaged. I used this to explain this one concept to the teachers: If we as educators can't agree on what is engaged, we are likely not giving a clear representation of what we need to see. Furthermore, the perception that there is one clear right or wrong is also faulty, which leads to more separation and frustration. The translation from what we want to see and what actually does impact academic outcomes is also less clear. For example, teachers may want parents to attend school functions, but there is no data that directly link attending the school play with having a better outcome for a child.

Defining the goals of engagement is an essential part of creating an effective parent and family engagement plan. The vision questions that you are answering at the end of each chapter are fine tuning what you hope to see if your program is successful. Ultimately, what you are visualizing is academic outcomes, personal opinions, community connections, and more. In this chapter, we will look at some of the perceptions, attitudes, and behaviors that we want to increase or decrease as a part of the parent engagement plan. A few of the products of strong engagement are listed below:

- Strong parent communication
- Teachers feeling supported
- Students successfully mastering academic standards
- Parents present in the building
- Strong community partnerships
- Healthy family units

In my work with schools, I begin by asking all participants some basics about engagement. Beyond what they do or don't know, I want to see some of the underlying emotional connections that impact perceptions. Much of what we build in relationships comes from perceptions. Referring back to the exercise that I described earlier, where teachers were asked to determine the level of engagement of the parents based on minimal information, consistently the teachers were split in their decisions. But when they were asked to describe *why* they had voted the way they voted, some came up with abstract concepts like intention and commitment, while others were more concerned with results and made their assumptions based upon what they believed the outcome would be. What one teacher felt was good intention another felt showed lack of commitment. Inconsistencies can lead to misunderstandings, miscommunications, and standards being unexpressed and unmet.

The second part of the training involved asking the teachers to describe specific activities that they wanted to see parents doing. Again, several themes were consistent. Most agreed with things like helping in the classroom, providing a consistent space for homework, and sharing community with other families. But when I gave some different scenarios that might come up, like a parent who is unable to pass the required background check or someone who is homebound due to a disability, and asked how they might be able to show support for their child and the school, I was met with fewer responses. What I wanted them to consider was that if we are the experts, then we have to come up with not only the problems but also some solutions.

The important takeaway is that when establishing your program, creating the vision allows you to have an anchor that makes your action more intentional. It's like a recipe; when you get ready to cook, you decide first what you want it to look like at the end, then you work your way back to the recipe, which tells you which ingredients you need. You wouldn't take out 10 random ingredients and then decide to make a meal; you choose the meal and then the components. When we start planning parent events, we do the opposite. We pick random events and hope that they will end up with parents who are capable of supporting their children and engaged. When done correctly, establishing your goals will lead naturally to the plan. As a counselor, I create treatment plans that should produce the desired results. If I have a student who struggles with self-control, we would learn about controlling our mind and body and maybe practice with an activity like bubble freeze, where students need to maintain complete stillness while I blow bubbles all around them. Teachers do the same thing; if they want to teach a math concept or literacy component, they plan a lesson to teach, reteach, and show mastery of the concept. Parent events, programming, and activities must be designed around the skills we want to teach, either those requested by parents or determined to be necessary by the assessments given to the students.

There are a variety of goals that you will want to consider. Taking into consideration the staff concerns is a reasonable place to start; it's important to remember, however, that only using subjective data will give you only subjective results. As you are creating your goals, begin by answering three key questions:

- What are we doing?
- Is it working?
- What do we want to do?

*As a side note, your school improvement plan may be a great place to get data for your vision. The goals for the overall school are an important piece of the puzzle as well.

In some school settings, a robust parent and teacher organization of some type creates the impression that parents are engaged. With support from administrators and with various activities, fundraisers, and volunteer duties being carried out, it's easy to assume that parents who participate are essentially engaged. To some extent this is indeed true; however, many of these schools still struggle with test scores or teachers who feel unappreciated all but one week of the year and students who may or may not be making the mark, so to speak. Additionally, some of the most active parents find themselves being overwhelmed or overworked trying to meet all of the needs that the school presents.

From the collaborative care framework, the goals should include not only the outcomes we hope to see for our own classrooms, hallways, and cafeterias but also what we hope to accomplish in the lives of our students and families in the community. For instance, as a school, your goal may be to increase reading scores for your students. It's not a difficult leap to expect that this will also benefit the students and families long term. However, in order to know exactly what areas you should focus on in your parent engagement efforts, you need two distinct pieces of information: what the students need help with and how to support the parents in helping them. This could range from needing extra books and resources in the home to needing adult education classes to help parents with reading skills of their own. To accomplish this, you might need the help of community social service agencies or volunteer college students to staff a tutoring program. The goals of the program are still to increase reading scores, but there may be additional preliminary goals you have to achieve in order to have complete success. Your formal plan helps you identify all of the areas to which you need to direct attention.

Vision

Which of the following goals are you hoping to achieve with the improvement of the parent engagement program?

- Strong parent communication
- Teachers feeling supported
- Students successfully mastering academic standards
- Parents present in the building
- Strong community partnerships
- Healthy family units

Plan

- Which goal will you focus on first?
- Who will lead this effort? If you have the ability to establish a team devoted to this effort that is best, particularly for the first year or two of the improvement efforts.
- Considering in-school time; out-of-school time; and parents, staff, and students, create a list of possible activities that will achieve the desired goals.

Action

- What progress-monitoring method will you use to assess your effectiveness toward the goal?
- How often will you progress monitor your goal?
- Assign tasks to each participant on the parent engagement team with specific deadlines for completion.

Notes/Brainstorming

Communication   4

The most important thing in communication is hearing what isn't being said.

—Anonymous

The foundation for successful engagement is a mutual respect and understanding between schools and families. Effective exchange of information is essential for this process. Most educators who feel that they are being successful base that perception at least in part on healthy communication exchanges. Those who feel that they could improve feel that way in part, generally, because of failed or strained communication.

A reasonable question I've often asked is why then do we spend so little time on teaching and developing effective communication? There is no real reason to assume that people are born with the skills to communicate well, and our education system does an incredible job at creating walls that hinder our communication. There are two foundational pieces of good communication: personal expression and listening for understanding.

When done well, personal expression can allow an individual to feel both connected and free. The act of exchanging information occurs when personal expression is met with listening for understanding. In an exchange, there is both a source and a receiver, and their willingness to give and receive is a positive influence in the process of communicating. In moments when expression is met with effective listening, the connection between two individuals can be very powerful. As educators, we receive training on how to deliver content and curriculum to students; we even learn about the way the age and developmental stage of children can impact the way in which they learn or interpret what we are trying to teach them. From that point, we may even go on to learn more about how to teach students with learning challenges. That is all about delivering information. The exchange of information is on what we need to work.

ACTIVE LISTENING

As a counselor, active listening is one of the tools I learned first and constantly work to master. Some professionals use the term "reflective listening," and both are designed to convey that simply hearing the words that an individual is saying does very little to convey that they are being understood. Active listening refers to understanding what is being said, paraphrasing, and responding empathically to what has been heard.

Simple reflection refers to restating what has been said. For example, when you have a student who says, "You never listen to me," you might say, "You think I haven't heard you." Using different words, you convey what has been said. In counseling, we also use something called "minimal encouragers," which are cues for the speaker to continue with what they are saying by giving some feedback that they are being heard without giving a direct response. Some examples include the following:

- A head nod
- Smiles
- Leaning into the conversation
- Using phrases like "mm hmm" or "I see"

The next level goes a little deeper: to respond by also acknowledging the underlying feeling of what is being said. So in this example, you might respond, "You're frustrated, because you don't feel heard." This can help, particularly when emotions are high and you're trying to diffuse a difficult situation.

It's important to also know what reflective listening is *not*:

- It is *not* solution finding.
- It is *not* agreement.
- It is *not* confrontation.
- It is *not* judgment.

The trouble with communication is that it can be so subjective. It is tempered with our individual experiences and shaped by our culture. Everything from tone and inflection of voice to slang and verbal jargon to body language are all considered forms of communication. By effectively using good communication, relationships are built, partnerships forged, and commitments are strengthened. Use faulty communication, and with limited contact relationships begin to seem less stable and rocky relationships can crumble.

Recently, in one of the Facebook groups of which I am a part, there was a discussion about the term "pushing in." I was surprised that one of the counselors who is also in the group stated that he was unfamiliar with the term. It surprised me because in my area, this is a commonly used term for any student with special education services who receives those services in the classroom rather than in a self-contained classroom. What struck me most about the thread was that in different areas of the country, even in different buildings near each other, the terms or acronyms that are used can vary wildly. It is important that we not ignore this fact when working with parents. Anything from who does what in the building to what certain terms mean may not be common knowledge for parents, and many may not feel comfortable interjecting to ask questions when we are going through our regular routine spiels. Look at the following terms and consider them as not well known when you are working with parents:

RTI—response to intervention

IEP—Individualized Education Plan

SPED—special education department

AP—assistant principal or Advanced Placement

PBIS—Positive Behavioral Interventions and Supports

Interventions—specialized techniques to address student challenges; can be academic or behavioral

ABA—applied behavior analysis

ASD—autism spectrum disorder

NCLB—No Child Left Behind Act of 2001; signed into law to ensure all children receive quality education

LRE—least restrictive environment; relates to classroom placement of special education students

Accommodations—adjustments to standard classwork made for students who receive special education services

ADHD—Attention-Deficit/Hyperactivity Disorder; a medical diagnosis that can be given by a trained professional and relates to behaviors exhibited by the child

Common Core—state-accepted standards for academic proficiency; not currently accepted by all states

School psychologist—school professional who conducts testing for special education classification; may also provide interventions

School counselor—school professional who supports student development in academic, social, and vocational areas; may also provide interventions

Instructional assistant—school professional who assists licensed teachers with instructing students; may assist with delivery of accommodations

DIVERSIFY COMMUNICATION

Do communicate unto others as they need communication done unto them.

—Pamela Jett

When I began my direct school-based work, I often provided surveys to determine the best practices for communication. In particular, I was looking for what methods of communication that schools had found, or even developed, to be most effective with our most communication-challenged families. You know the ones I'm talking about. The parents who have four different phone numbers with no voicemails set up, but who wouldn't call you even if you did leave a message. The parents who see your number and push decline. The parents who've never seen that newsletter you spend an hour on every week nor opened it via e-mail. These types of issues can be all too common, but finding working solutions can be much more difficult.

One of the ways we can problem solve is by diversifying our communication strategies. Most educators are comfortable with one or two methods that they use regularly; however, from year to year what your parents are actually using may change. In her article "Making the Most of Back-to-School Communications," Anne O'Brien was really clear on the goal of taking back-to-school to the next level (O'Brien, 2015). O'Brien suggested thinking outside of the box, or at least outside of the building, by having veteran educators and administrators spending time in the community during the back-to-school season in voluntary and promotional opportunities. She also recommended six shares. All positive content should be shared in six unique ways. This means that it is not enough to simply create the blog post and expect parents to find it. It is not appropriate to send home a paper newsletter and do nothing else. Having content delivered multiple times and in multiple ways gives us a greater chance for acknowledgment and accessibility by parents.

Here's an exciting concept that I have begun recommending. I learned about it on the blog Diary of a Not So Wimpy Teacher; she calls it the Friday journal (Sears, 2015). In short, she has her students write a letter to parents once a week, on Friday, about what they learned during the week or what they were excited about for the upcoming week. This idea is awesome for a couple reasons. First, she noticed about 50 percent effectiveness over her traditional paper communication methods. Not bad, but not what she wanted. So with this, she is able to make sure the kids are excited to show the message rather than losing the traditional newsletter before they get home. But, the second point, which I think I like more, is that because it is personal from the kids, parents are more interested, and it serves as a conversation starter as well. Let's not even begin to think about the literacy standards and such. It's just an amazing way to incorporate a lens of engagement without making life more difficult for teachers. The kids are doing the work. Genius!

PHONE COMMUNICATION

Communicating over the phone is really becoming a lost art in our modern technologically driven society. Many people do not even maintain a "landline," and it's not uncommon for us to more commonly text or e-mail than speak over the phone. While the same communication strategies can be used regardless of method of communication, there are a few tips that can also be applied to the conversations that parents and teachers have.

Parent Communication Tips

Most educators will agree that there is very little that is more stressful than having to deliver less-than-pleasant information to parents. However, at some point of the school year, you will likely have the need to call a parent with what may be news they don't want to hear. Hopefully, you have already had a positive conversation with the family so that the relationship has been established, but even if you haven't, there are some things you can do to make the conversation go a little smoother. Here are a few tips to get you started.

Be clear before you dial. Jot down a few notes or key points that you need to be sure to communicate. Check them off as you go so that you have a record of the information that you shared. It's easy to get off track; having an anchor is helpful.

Introduce yourself. Sounds simple enough, but parents who have multiple children or are in a stressful situation may not connect with your name. A simple, "This is Mrs. Smith. I wanted to talk to you about Ben," will suffice.

Ask if this is a good time. Most people skip this step, but I think it goes a long way with most parents. Many parents answer their phones at work and will be concerned about missing pay or losing their jobs for talking too long. If you want them to be fully present in the conversation, make sure you offer them that courtesy of having the conversation at a different time. If, in fact, this is not a good time, give them a brief overview such as, "I wanted to speak with you about Jane's math grade. When is a good time to talk?" This ensures that you have touched on at least a portion of your to-do list, while respecting the fact that they cannot speak at length. Some parents may make time for a conversation at this point, others may be less inclined to return your call at all; it is a risk you run, but I think that it is a great place to start when you hope to have a collaborative conversation.

Use the sandwich approach. Unless you are giving the brief overview mentioned in tip three, when at all possible start with something positive, then move to the negative, and end with a positive statement or call to action. An example would be, "JayShawn has made some big improvements in his math, and I'm very proud of his effort. Unfortunately, he seems to still have trouble in reading, and I think some additional reading time would help him a lot. Would that be something you would consider?"

Listen and, if necessary, be willing to adjust. Your plan for the child may or may not be the best, but parents who feel heard will always be more willing to agree and follow through than those who feel a sentence has been imposed on them or their child. Remember, parents may be defensive as a method of "protecting" their child, even when you are not trying to hurt them. Listening will allow them to see that you not only value their opinion but you might come up with an even better solution than you had originally planned.

Be specific and clear. Saying things like "He needs to read more at home" isn't as helpful as "I would like him to read to you for 15 minutes each night." Don't assume that when parents aren't doing things you think they should be doing that they know how to do them. Often, parents are doing the best that they know how to, and with specific instructions, you can make good progress.

Look for the win-win solution. Difficult conversations can often turn into conflicts. Conflicts are really just opposing viewpoints of the same situation. Even if you don't agree, there are typically ways to have both parties walk away with a mutually agreed-upon plan. Identify the main goal for each party and then go from there. Since both parties want the child to succeed, use that as a great place to start. Sometimes you'll have to brainstorm a list of possible solutions to find which ones will work, but ultimately parents are more likely to follow through on solutions in which they are invested. For our students we want progress, not perfection. Your plan may be the perfect one, but if the parents won't support the student doing it for some reason, that won't matter much.

Do send a follow-up e-mail or note home. For particularly detailed conversations, it is nice to send a wrap-up e-mail or summary. I say, "I'm going to send you an e-mail to review what we discussed. Let me know if you have any questions after you read it." The details of education are common to us, but the language, connotation, and, more importantly, the meaning of the words that we say can be lost on parents. Sometimes they will agree and not fully understand. Just like our kiddos, some of them are visual learners or need to read to themselves to fully grasp content, or perhaps they have more questions after the information has settled. Sending the follow-up gives them permission to keep the dialogue going, which is always good.

Monitor your tone and body language. Our emotions are rarely hidden. Particularly when we are heading into a stressful situation, our tone and body language might be unconsciously giving off the impression that we are ready for a fight. Take deep breaths and monitor your tone and rate of speech; it will help you project only what you want to get across.

TACKLING COMMUNICATION PROBLEMS

Have you ever called a parent and gotten no answer, left a message, and never gotten a response? Have you had a great meeting with a parent, come up with a perfect plan, and then not gotten any follow-through? Do you spend time each week crafting a newsletter only to find out that the parents who needed it most never actually saw it? If any of these seem like common occurrences in your life, you are not alone. Communication challenges are one of the primary concerns when I work with educators.

A while ago, I attended a professional development session by Pamela Jett, a respected communication expert, titled, "Not Everyone Was Raised in Your House." Isn't that catchy? The focus of the session was improving communication in all forms. The premise was that in communication much is implied, and our perception of word meaning has much to do with connotation, historical context, body language, vocal tone, and mood. Communication between schools or educators and parents can easily be strained, and I think a great deal of it is exactly because of what Pamela was inferring: Our world views are related to everything from the homes we grew up in to the way we perceive what is going on around us. One thing that never ceases to amaze me, as a mother of four children, is how I, as one person, can be involved in a situation with all of my children and have one perspective and each of them can have a completely different perspective on the exact same event. The same is true in my work with families. I was in a family team meeting recently with a client of mine and her ex-husband. The ex-husband, we'll call him James, was sitting on one side of the table, tattooed from head to toe, cursing like a sailor, and alluding to his "rough" life. His mother and siblings were on the other side of the table, looking very presentable, calm, and collected. These four people, living in the same home, had completely different experiences and outcomes. All of them had been exposed to similar traumatic events but the impact on each of them was different.

Even if you had a similar childhood to the parents with whom you are trying to connect, their perception of that childhood could be completely different. Assumptions can work for or against us in communication, so we need to be careful and aware. When a parent walks into the classroom for a conference, we often make assumptions, sometimes correctly, about how we should communicate, but understanding that our perceptions could be wrong will allow us to have room for adjustment and will go a long way toward addressing communication barriers.

ELECTRONIC COMMUNICATION

Most teachers have become proficient in using some type of electronic means of communication and we'll share some of the tools used later, but most could use a little tune-up to maximize the effects of their effort. Figure 4.1 is a copy of an e-mail sent out by a kindergarten teacher to parents during the first week of school.

Figure 4.1 E-mail Sample 1

Good Evening Parents and Families!

I heard about everyone's weekend from the children and it sounds like you enjoyed the weekend despite the rainy weather we had! My fiancée and I spent the day Saturday with my parents, younger brothers, and grandpa at the Indiana State Fair. This is the flrst time I have been to the state fair and able to walk around without a knee walker or a wheelchair, so it was pretty awesome! I really enjoy eating fair food and looking at all the vendors in the Expo Hall, very exciting stuff, and thankfully the rain held off while we were there! My dog, Charlie, even got a little homemade dog treat from one of the vendors! He was excited! I was even more excited to share my photos of the animals I saw with the kids! It was so fun looking at photos of cows and pigs today!

This week we will continue learning our procedures in the classroom and the school, also focusing on more specific procedures. We will learn about letters A–E, how to spell the colors (red, yellow, blue, green, and orange), and the numbers 1–5. The students began using their Writing Folders today, which means we have begun writing our first class book! You will be able to see some photos of us creating the book on our Twitter page this week! We had a lot of fun coming up with a title for our class book and we will vote on it tomorrow based on the choices we have. I will start the year by doing a class writing activity, and then the next book the children make will be their choice and individualized to them. I will send all these stories home with the children at the end of the first trimester, but you will be able to see them during Parent Teacher Conferences in the fall. ☺ This week, I will introduce their Math Notebooks. Each day, after we have our math mini lesson, the students will be asked to answer a math problem in their math journal, which they will paste into their journal and then write or draw a picture to answer the question. This will also encourage the students to write and think about their thinking and how they are solving math problems, instead of just solving them. ☺

As you saw in their red folders, the only homework this week will be for your children to read. They are able to read for as long as you (and them) are willing and able to each night, but I have a goal for 10–15 minutes each night! The children are able to read you the book (either by looking at the words, pictures, or retelling a familiar story page by page), you may read to them, or they can read with a friend or sibling. I have taken note that this particular class of students LOVES books, so I think this will be an easy homework assignment. Please turn in this homework on Monday, August 17 (signed by you with the amount of minutes read during the week) and after your child has 4 (FOUR) reading assignments turned in, they will be able to choose a prize from the treasure box for all their hard work! I will be sending home a project on Friday for you to complete with your child and family members to help the other students in the class (and myself) learn a little bit more . . .

I have been kind enough to block out the name of the sender and recipients. But if you saw the original, you would note that this text-rich e-mail had a scroll bar, meaning that the three paragraphs that you see are only about half of the e-mail. How effective do you think this e-mail is at engaging parents? Nothing about this encourages me to read, take note of, or even be interested in the content. What I think about most is that if

I am a parent with literacy issues or who does not speak English, opening this e-mail might prompt me to be anxious or frustrated. I'm sure the intention was to relay as much information as possible so that parents are informed, but unfortunately it does quite the opposite.

By contrast, see Figure 4.2.

Note the simple bullet points, dates and times of importance highlighted, and most importantly, limited content. Mentally, as I open this, I am more inclined to finish reading the e-mail because I believe the content to be relevant.

End lesson, keep e-mail simple and easy to read. Many families have limited Internet access and each e-mail they open on their phone requires them to pay more on their cell phone bill. Is the information you're sending important enough to pay for? Well we hope so, but making it easy to digest helps everyone. I also like the idea of using some pictures or other visual representation of material presented in e-mails, since not all parents have the same literacy abilities. Working in a school where much of the 70 percent of my families who speak Spanish don't read Spanish or English, a lengthy e-mail full of only words may not even get a glance. Bulleted material in simple words has a better chance of getting through to the recipients.

Another strategy Anne O'Brien suggested in her article "Making the Most of Back-to-School Communication" is the flipped classroom concept. It involves sending out curriculum or content in advance and then having students bring questions to class. The same can be done for meetings, events, or discussions with parents. Sending out the information saves time and gives those who need more time to process information time to

| Figure 4.2 | E-mail Sample 2 |

Good morning!

Here are some reminders of upcoming events:

- Wednesday, June 3rd: Study trip to Indianapolis Art Museum (IMA). We will board the buses at 9:30 to head to the museum and will leave the museum at 2:00. Students and chaperones need a sack lunch in a disposable bag . . . no lunch boxes, please. Dress for the weather, we plan to eat outside and be at the 100 Acre park in the afternoon.
- Friday, June 5th: Field Day (during specials class time)
- Friday, June 5th: FCPA Summer Festival from 6:00–8:00. Please come down to Community 2 to see our class's animal research projects on display.
- Tuesday, June 9th: Last day for students!

do just that. So keep in mind, e-mail communication does not have to be your sole source of content. Use it more frequently to deliver short bursts. To summarize, here are a couple dos and don'ts:

- Do keep e-mails short and simple.
- Do use "BCC" or another method of hiding parent e-mail addresses unless they have given you permission to share.
- Do include pictures when possible.
- Don't have difficult conversations over e-mail.
- Don't use all caps or excessive punctuation.
- Don't forget "tone" is extremely subjective in e-mails; they are best for facts and not emotions.

Recently, I was looking for information on school policy about whether or not to send a child to school. Working on attendance as a chronic issue in schools, I was sure that I would find a list of what to look for to tell me if my child was sick enough to stay home. I went to several different websites and was not able to locate anything that concretely listed conditions that should prevent a child from being sent to school. As a parent with a potentially sick child, would I really spend 10 minutes looking for this list? No. Would I spend 10 minutes calling to find a sitter and leave the child home? Maybe. Would I assume that the child is not sick enough to stay home and send him or her to school ill? Possibly. All of this means the same thing: If you want parents to have the information, you have to be giving it to them often and in a variety of ways. Otherwise, there's really no reason to complain about it not getting received.

Creating electronic newsletters is a great way to increase the visual appeal of your e-mail information. Have you ever used the website Smore .com? See in Figure 4.3 two documents that I created in about 20 minutes with some quick tips for parents.

A couple things you will notice. First, this is a school that is 70 percent native Spanish speakers. Translating was not an option for me; it was essential. While not all parents who speak Spanish read Spanish, it is a good skill for our students who are learning to read to also know how to read Spanish. It's both respectful of their native language and practical, as well as being culturally acceptable to begin translating as a young child in many families. If a child is reading the newsletter to a parent, they are building multiple skills. Second, I used visuals to which families would automatically be drawn. Pictures of our students and classroom bulletin boards also offer a glimpse into school life for parents who may not be readily aware of what goes on in our building.

Figure 4.3 Smore Newsletter Sample

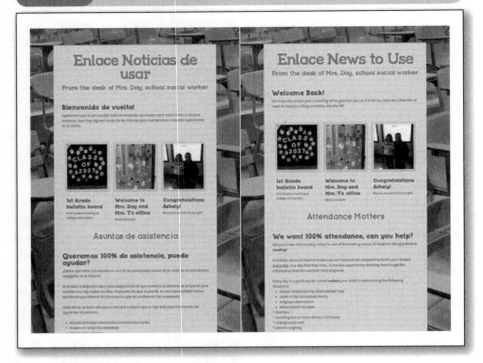

NEWSLETTERS AND PARENT COMMUNICATION

Regular parent communication is always important in any parent engagement plan. However, newsletters sometimes fail to gain the momentum that teachers hope for because they don't make it home or are not read by the parents at all. For many parents, checking the backpack is a routine, but for others it is one more thing on a long to-do list that is not helpful. The following sections are tools that can be used to make the common newsletter methods more interesting.

MAILCHIMP

MailChimp is a free e-mail template service that allows users free access to send e-mails with customized content to subscribers. There are a variety of tools to make e-mails engaging with social network links, and the best part is that the service is free. For up to 2,000 e-mail addresses, much more than a teacher will likely ever need, you can have access to this free tool. In many ways, MailChimp is easier and more effective than traditional e-mail. The drag-and-drop method lends itself well to providing visual content, which is more interactive for families. The free service also allows you to monitor not only who opened the e-mail, but when they opened it and whether or not they clicked any of the links you provided. Another great feature is that unlike traditional e-mails, which generally publish all of the e-mails together, each individual e-mail is sent with no BCC or CC, so there is no unnecessary exchange of information.

HARNESSING THE POWER OF SOCIAL MEDIA

It may seem strange that I am discussing the subject of social media in a book about parent engagement, but I want you to be aware of all the tools you can add to your toolbox. Many schools have discovered the benefit of social media in communicating with parents and students. Unfortunately, few have discovered how to use it effectively. In many instances, schools have relatively unvisited social media pages with limited followers. Educators struggle to come up with relevant content that both engages families and shares the information we hope to get delivered.

As a school counselor, I have the ability to provide in-class lessons for students. During a recent lesson, I came up with the bright idea of having my students post pictures of the take-home activity that I gave them. With the simple promise of a prize, literally no details about what they would win, the kids were excited to share with their parents, and the parents were happy to post. As is customary on the page that I manage, the post gained engagement of about 250 people, which is equal to the number of families we have in our building.

Not only did I make sure that the information that I wanted to get to parents got there, it allowed the parents to engage in a conversation about the resources I provide. We also gained more followers on our social media platforms, which is one of my favorite ways to communicate with parents regularly. By scaffolding communication in this way, I am more likely to include a parent or two who may not have gotten the information, and it requires nothing additional on my part.

It is important to note that data on the impact of social media are emerging, and there is an apparent divide between social classes, race, and locations that has yet to be clarified. However, as more professionals become comfortable with the technology, the potential is endless. In some instances, families with limited means have more access to social media than they do to traditional e-mail or standard voice calls. In addition, the use of the parent-teacher chat, which was designed to connect educators, parents, and school-based professionals to communicate over a topic moderated by a leader in engagement strategies, has been found to create quick and efficient dialogue among stakeholders.

I have specifically included a section about social media, with full knowledge that many schools are opposed to using this tool. But regardless of the potential backlash from those not supportive, it is in fact just that, a tool. And used correctly, it can be an incredibly powerful one. The number of registered and regular users of social media far outreaches the access of regular use of electronic mail by certain demographics. By choosing not to use social media, there can be exclusion by default.

The concern over social media is relevant as educators, particularly those working with older students, see the harm caused by anything from reckless posting to cyberbullying. In addition, some parents who oppose the use of social media by their children are less likely to be active on the different sites themselves. Below we'll explore some of the pros and cons and best practices by looking at the different options with social media.

Facebook

Established in 2004 by a group of college cohorts, most notably Mark Zuckerberg, Facebook's origin and original intent has been up for debate. What is clear is that with over 1.28 billion active monthly users and over 50 million pages, it has become one of the most popular pastimes and has revolutionized the way society functions as a whole. It is one of the top marketing tools used by business professionals to quickly get in front of potential customers. For schools, the number 57 is important. This is the percentage of American adults who say that they check social media at least once per day. This is higher than the percentage that checks their e-mail, more than the number that checks their voicemail, and we're not even going to discuss how infrequently some parents check backpacks for paper documents. The reality is that Facebook is an incredibly handy, FREE way to communicate quick bursts of content to parents. There are some tricks, however.

Because of the marketing capability, Facebook continuously updates its posting algorithms so that the content displayed on a user's newsfeed is engaging enough to keep them scrolling. The exact measures that Facebook programmers use are strictly under lock and key and change regularly, but I can tell you they do not work in the favor of those who only occasionally post. For many businesses, they have seen a dramatic decrease in users engaging with their page because Facebook wants them to pay a premium for boosting posts. Most schools don't have a line item in the budget for social media, but it may be worthwhile to spend some of the advertising dollars there. If, however, you don't have that spending luxury, there are still ways to get parents seeing more of what you post.

As part of the work that I do with schools, I sometimes manage social media posts. The reason for this is I want to make sure I am engaging parents on every platform that I can. I have been able to document engagement on our social media platforms of nearly equal proportions to our family population. This means that I have the same number of people actively engaged in our posts as I have families in our school. I have even seen the messages I post translate into real life as parents contact our office based upon something that they have seen online.

What this really means is the more you post, the more what you do is shown to people who like your page. The more visually appealing things you show, the more people will like or comment on your posts, which boosts the number of people to whom Facebook will show your content. Facebook wants people to "like" what you post, because the more people enjoy what they see on social media, the more advertisers will pay. If you have a post that performs well, they will help you and share it more frequently, so it becomes a win-win.

But I know what you're saying. You're saying, I don't have time to burn on finding new amazing content to engage families AND post about it 10 times a day. And you're right, you don't, so here's what you can do. You can empower your staff and students to post regularly and you can ask them to tag you as often as possible. If you have 10 teachers regularly posting and tagging and you make a habit once per day of engaging what they post, you've done all you need to do. In the following box, you will also see some sample postings for your social media campaigns (Garst, 2015).

SOCIAL MEDIA POST TEMPLATES

Questions

- What was your favorite school lunch?
- What was your favorite teacher's name?
- What was your child's homework tonight?
- What advice would you give to other parents about setting up a homework routine?
- What's your favorite family-friendly movie?

Contests

- We are offering free tickets to tonight's {basketball/softball/soccer} game. To enter, like and share this post.

(Continued)

(Continued)

- We are offering free tickets to tonight's musical. To enter, comment with your favorite musical.
- To win a free pizza dinner from {insert sponsor}, comment with your favorite pizza topping.
- To win a free movie from {insert sponsor}, comment with the first movie you ever saw in a theater.
- Post pictures of your building, then ask people what the picture shows.

Quotes

- "Live as if you were to die tomorrow. Learn as if you were to live forever."—Mahatma Gandhi
- "You can never be overdressed or overeducated."—Oscar Wilde
- "Education is the most powerful weapon which you can use to change the world."—Nelson Mandela
- "I did then what I knew how to do. Now that I know better, I do better."—Maya Angelou
- "Children must be taught how to think, not what to think."—Margaret Mead
- "Intelligence plus character—that is the goal of true education."—Martin Luther King Jr.
- "It does not matter how slowly you go as long as you do not stop."—Confucius
- "Educating the mind without educating the heart is no education at all."—Aristotle

Note: Creating visuals of your quotes is a great way to more actively engage social media users. Several tools exist to do that, including PicMonkey.com, Canva.com, and Quozio.com, among others. Fun quotes from students can also be used.

Holiday Ideas

- Name your favorite holiday treat.
- Which do you watch first, *The Grinch* or *The Santa Clause*?
- Did you know there is a National Belly Laugh Day? That's right, it's today! (January 24)
- Happy Earth Day! (April 22)
- It's National Parents' Day! Give yourself a break; you're doing an awesome job! (July 26)
- September 13 is National Grandparents Day. Have you called the grandparents in your life today?

Personal Posts from Staff

If any of your teachers have blogs, Facebook pages, or Twitter accounts, ask them to share their latest posts with you. Better yet, follow and share organically.

Twitter

For those of you unfamiliar with Twitter, here is a crash course. This website boasts that it is an "information network made up of 140-character messages called Tweets." The goal, like that of all social media, is to exchange information. To use Twitter, one must have a profile, which can consist of as much or as little information as you please but must include your profile name, which can be a version of your real name, that of your business, or something completely random. Figure 4.4 shows my profile.

As you can see, you have room for a profile picture, a header image, a brief bio, and your wall, which includes your tweets as well as tweets from people whom you follow. Twitter is also kind enough to show you people who you might enjoy following along the sidebar. You will also see a few numbers on the page. Your tweets; your "following" is the people with whom you have connected; your followers, or the people who have connected with you; and your favorites, or things you've marked with stars.

With regard to parent communication, you can create a personal profile or one for your classroom or department. Like Facebook, the challenge

Figure 4.4 Twitter Profile Sample

Source: Twitter.com.

is to get parents to engage with your profile, meaning they must follow you in order to get the maximum exposure for what you are sharing. But unlike Facebook, Twitter has this wonderful tool called a hashtag, which can be used to circumvent the pay-for-exposure feature. The hashtag (#) is added to a phrase not separated by spaces. For example, #backtoschool or #funfriday are hashtags. Because of the 140-character limit, you can also use things like #back2school to save on letters. When you are working on a particular topic, getting exposure is as simple as searching for the hashtag phrase, and you will get a running list of tweets containing that phrase. You can then retweet or chat with others who are engaging in a conversation.

Composing tweets can be tricky. The first step is figuring out what to tweet. Like on other platforms, videos and images do very well on Twitter. Snapshots from classrooms, pictures of extracurricular activities, or projects are also good starting points. The content can be questions, fun quotes, and helpful tips for families like local social service opportunities, free giveaways, or the latest in educational tools. I also encourage teachers to tweet pictures of exceptional work from within the classroom or while they are home grading. Student names can be excluded to comply with FERPA regulations and it's a great way to showcase what you are already doing. A quick tip on the 140-character limit: When you are attempting to send a link to another page, you will most likely want to shrink it since many links can include dozens of characters. There are several tools available to do this, including http://shrinkthislink.com/, http://ow.ly/url/shorten-url, and http://tinyurl.com/.

Facebook and Twitter aren't the only social media platforms that can be used to engage families. There are promising ways to connect developing all the time. I wouldn't invest tons of time as a primary strategy, but it can be an amazing complement to the overall program. There are more social media platforms beginning every day; below are a few more tips that can be used and applied across multiple platforms:

- Make a group Pinterest board and ask teachers to pin to it. Share pins that teachers are using or will use.
- For older grades, have them create an in-class page and decide on one group post each week.
- During meetings, take a few minutes at the beginning and ask parents to physically take out their phones and like your page or follow you on Twitter.
- Create QR codes, which are images that you scan with a smartphone or tablet computer to link with people socially.

- Run contests on social media for free admission to extracurricular events.
- Create a separate classroom on Remind.com for the school so you can text parents without giving out cell numbers.
- Ask parents to tag themselves in photos.
- Like and follow other education-minded pages, then share their content.
- A relatively new platform is Periscope, which allows you to take live videos and feed them out; use this as a method to show parents how to practice skills from your classroom or home.

The bottom line on communication is that without it, you will fail at engaging families. If there has not been a review of communication systems and routines, that should occur sooner rather than later and include perspectives from all parties on the level of effectiveness. Start with a clear message and openness to exchange information, and prepare for all families by using a variety of strategies. The reflection questions in this section will give you an idea of some other areas to consider when looking at this part of your plan.

Vision

- What methods of communication are you regularly using? How are they working?
- If you are a classroom teacher, what ways can you use social media to communicate information to your parents or engage with them in dialogues? If you are not in the classroom, what methods do you use to get parents to interact with you electronically?
- How comfortable are you with the communication methods mentioned?

Plan

- Do district policies prevent you from using social media?
- Are there additional staff members, tools, or contractors needed to improve communication methods?
- Do staff members need additional training?
- Can the process of communication be looped into the curriculum? Can the student-run school paper also be sent to parents?
- Are there current software programs that have extension programs for parent communication?

(Continued)

(Continued)

Action

- Is parent communication included in all job descriptions?
- How is effective communication monitored in the parent-teacher relationship?
- Is the building- or district-level policy for communication effective?

Notes/Brainstorming

Program 5
Components

Programs designed with a strong parent component produce students who perform better than otherwise identical programs that do not involve parents as thoroughly or not at all.

—Anne T. Henderson

Now that you've gotten a strong grasp of some of the basics of engagement, let's take stock of the current activities that fall under the heading of parent engagement. The following should not be considered an all-inclusive list, as you may have more or fewer than these activities regularly occurring in your building. Check any that you know you have currently or add items that you have that may fall under this heading but aren't on this list. In the following section, we'll look at some innovative ways of improving upon these concepts in depth.

- Parent volunteer program
- Parent-teacher organization
- Parent council
- Parent resource center
- Parent website/portal
- Teacher or school blogs
- Parent demonstration events (career days, etc.)
- Multifaceted communication
- Donation request board
- Parent breakfasts
- Parent dinners
- Parent workshops
- Family-friendly board meetings
- Community-based family nights
- Culturally responsible staff
- Home visits
- Parent recognition tools
- Teacher training
- Parent leadership training
- Family orientation events
- Needs assessment for staff

So how did you do? Most schools have at least half of these occurring regularly in their building in some way or another. Some individual classrooms have this as well. Depending on your population, half may be all you need to have well-informed, active parents. In some settings however, you may need all of these and then some. It's less important where you start than where you're going. Knowing your starting point gives a foundation for your plan.

We've talked at length about surveying parents for their input and desires related to programming. Now we'll look a little deeper at another foundation piece, the needs assessment. Similar to survey data, the needs assessment looks at big-picture items that the classroom teacher or school leadership want to address and takes into consideration all of the variables that may be impacting the topic. Most people are really clear that they want engaged parents and families, but as they look at the current system they are less clear about what needs to be changed or is missing. The process of assessing is a multifaceted approach that includes self-reflection and student and community input.

One of the first steps that I take when working with schools is to begin with a brief staff survey. Designed to give me direct insight into the school climate, I use questions that assess knowledge, perceptions, and intentions. I believe that it is important for these results to be anonymous so fear does not impact responses. A sample of the personal needs assessment that I provided to schools as a part of this process is included here. It is advised that this be administered electronically so that teachers are able to be fully candid. Ensuring honest responses is more important than pinpointing one or two people who are not committed. Typically, those people will reveal themselves sooner or later, so for this portion of the assessment process, it's not important to know exactly who said what.

Figure 5.1 is a template of a teacher survey I have schools complete prior to providing professional development for staff on the topic of parent engagement and some of the results we saw. These questions can be modified to include or exclude data that you deem relevant, but see results from two districts that I worked with during the summer of 2015. I generally lean toward making the survey brief and gaining the minimum amount of information to encourage participants to complete the information. You can include other data if you choose, including topics like how many hours teachers typically spend communicating with parents, how comfortable they are with completing home visits, or how they document what they do to engage families.

In my book *Drag 'Em Kicking and Screaming*, there is a chapter titled "Educator, Know Thyself." This concept is really based upon the earliest classes in my school counseling program when my instructors were very clear

Figure 5.1 Teacher Survey Sample

1. What is your role in the school?

   - Teacher
   - Administrator
   - Support staff
   - Other

2. How long have you worked in education?

   - 1 year or less
   - 1–5 years
   - 6–10 years
   - 11–15 years
   - 16+ years

3. Rate the amount of "pre-service" training you received on engaging parents in education.

   This can be in your formal education or independent training.

1	2	3	4	5	6	7	8	9	10

   None/poor quality   Tons/exceptional quality

4. How much professional development have you received on parent engagement?

   - 10 hours or less
   - 11–20 hours
   - 21–30 hours
   - 31+ hours

5. Does your school have a parent engagement plan?

   - Yes
   - No
   - Not sure

6. What is your role in your school's parent engagement plan?

7. What are the components of Epstein's framework on parent engagement? Check all that apply.

   - Parenting
   - Communication
   - Volunteering
   - Learning
   - Decision Making
   - Community Collaboration
   - Relationship
   - Other:

(Continued)

Figure 5.1 (Continued)

8. How comfortable are you with parent communication in difficult situations?

   1   2   3   4   5   6   7   8   9   10
   Not comfortable at all; very stressful   Extremely comfortable; very prepared

9. How comfortable are you with parents who have limited English language?

   1   2   3   4   5   6   7   8   9   10
   Not comfortable at all; very stressful   Extremely comfortable; very prepared

10. How comfortable are you with parents being a part of your classroom?

    1   2   3   4   5   6   7   8   9   10
    Not comfortable at all; very stressful   Extremely comfortable; very prepared

11. How comfortable are you with trying new strategies to engage parents?

    1   2   3   4   5   6   7   8   9   10
    Not comfortable at all; very stressful   Extremely comfortable; very prepared

12. How supported do you feel by parents in your school?

    1   2   3   4   5   6   7   8   9   10
    Not supported at all   Extremely supported

13. How do you evaluate the engagement of parents in your classroom?

14. In your opinion, how well does your SCHOOL engage families?

    1   2   3   4   5   6   7   8   9   10
    Not well; limited attention on   Extremely well; lots of attention on
    engaging families   engaging families

15. In your opinion, how well does your DISTRICT engage families?

    1   2   3   4   5   6   7   8   9   10
    Not well; limited attention on   Extremely well; lots of attention on
    engaging families   engaging families

16. In your opinion, how well do YOU engage families?

    1   2   3   4   5   6   7   8   9   10
    Not well; limited attention on   Extremely well; lots of attention on
    engaging families   engaging families

17. How often do you include parents as decision makers in your classroom?

    1   2   3   4   5
    Never   Regularly

18. How many ways do you regularly communicate with families? Check all that apply.

- Phone (voice)
- Phone (text)
- E-mail (direct)
- E-mail (newsletter)
- Facebook
- Twitter
- Blog
- Home visits
- Paper newsletter
- Other:

19. Describe an engaged parent in your own words.

20. Please share any questions or comments you have after completing this survey.

Please include any areas you would like more information about or specific situations (without names) that you would like used in a training session.

21. How many professional development hours would you be willing to devote to training on parent engagement?

- Less than 1 hour
- 1–4 hours
- 5–8 hours
- 9–16 hours

that we all naturally carry biases, which can be very influential in the way in which we interact with students and/or clients. My goal with the exercises is that ignoring these biases or blind spots does very little to benefit anyone. Acknowledging, even with limited adjustment, can be extremely helpful.

Whenever possible, I give this or a version of this prior to professional development delivery. When I am able to, I temper the session to the results that I receive. Notice that we are assessing all six areas highlighted in Epstein's framework. Some teachers are either naturally or intentionally better in certain areas and not as strong in others. The goal for this is to establish data points for personal growth. It is important to ensure that these data are not used in a punitive fashion, as it can skew results when participants are afraid their honesty will be harmful to their professional standing. Anonymity helps with that, but also making sure that administration is in agreement with preventing punishment for "bad" results is important as well.

During a recent session of professional development, I delivered to a local K–eighth grade charter in Indianapolis. I asked teachers to help me brainstorm a list of potential ways that parents can volunteer in the building, out of the building, and in the home. This particular school had what I considered to be limited participation in the pre-survey. From the responses I did receive, one of the areas that I noted was that teachers didn't always feel supported by parents, but there were limited specific examples. What I wanted to do with this session was help teachers establish actionable points. These are the points that are clear and show success or weakness of the programming. Because of the area where the school was located and the demographics of the population, which included a significant number of families living in poverty, the challenges to engagement can be varied. I was specific in saying "in-school, out-of-school, and at home," because it is possible that parents who want to support school activities may not be able to pass background checks. In an effort to remove barriers, providing ideas that parents can participate in without having to pass the background check encourages them to be involved. In Figure 5.2, you see a sample of the bookmarks that can be given out at parent events asking parents to consider giving the school a hand with a variety of tasks. This can be customized to include additional enrichment activities that schools want to promote. For older students, you might use a punch card and allow them to turn it in for free entrance to a sporting event. The idea is to be as specific as possible, which removes a barrier for parents trying to think of what to do and frees up the teachers who may not have time once school starts to stop what they are doing long enough to ask. As a bonus, asking parents to commit to completing a certain level of engagement during the year actually encourages consistency and promotes extra help. When incentivized, you may even find parents requesting the cards to complete multiples.

From your needs assessment you can determine areas where skills may need to be improved. Perhaps you notice the majority of your teachers are only using one or two methods of communication with limited success; you may need to give them a brief in-service on how to use the technology. In another situation, you may notice that some of your teachers are very uncomfortable with communicating with families who speak languages other than English; you may not be able to make them all bilingual, but anything from making more translators available to helping them with the anxiety that they feel may improve communication with those families. The point is that your professional development must be intentional.

Figure 5.2 Sample Bookmarks

FRONT

Can you give us a hand?

We can use your help! On the back of bookmark, we've got a list of ideas to get you started, but if there's something else you want to do to help our school be the BEST, please let us know!

In as little as five minutes, YOU can make a difference!

BACK

- Attend field trip
- Sponsor a club
- Attend school events
- Read with a student
- Attend board meetings
- Help teachers with tasks
- Donate classroom snacks
- Bring your kids to school every day
- Visit the library
- Attend community events
- Clean up after events
- Talk with your child about school
- Encourage other parents
- Request donations for the school

81

PROFESSIONAL DEVELOPMENT WITH INTENTIONALITY

When I reach out to schools about providing them with professional development about parent engagement, very often what they really want is for me to come in and fix the parents. They want me to give them a magic potion that will make all the parents engage in all the programs and initiatives that the school has to offer, and they want the parents to appreciate and support the school and/or teacher. Well, I don't have a magic wand and, as much as I would like to make sure that all educators are well respected and don't have to deliver pizza on the weekend to pay student loans, the reality is that's not what professional development can do. What good-quality professional development CAN do is begin to uncover hidden barriers subconsciously reinforced by educators and shine a light on the ways in which educators can make the process of engaging in education more appealing to parents. See below some data I received when

---

Figure 5.3 Sample Professional Development Data

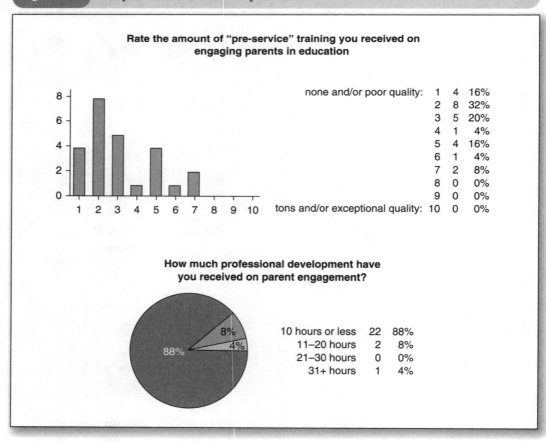

polling educators about the training that they have received related to parental engagement.

It is reasonable to assume, based upon this information, that *these* teachers have not had an appropriate amount of education on the subject of parent engagement. However, these teachers are a reasonable representation of the greater sum total of teachers. Most teachers have limited parent engagement experiences built into their educations, and very little direct professional development time is spent specifically on engaging families.

One organization seeking to change that fact is The Harvard Family Research Project (HFRP). HFRP is an educational powerhouse in the world of parent engagement. They recognized years ago that there was a need for educators to receive additional training on the subject of engaging families, and since that time they have been one of the leaders in providing quality instruction and professional development. While focusing on educating educators, HFRP has spent a great deal of energy on research and development of which we are able to make use. The research that they have conducted strongly supports what I have found in providing professional development, which is that educators want to engage families but often lack appropriate training to do so effectively. One of the most important aspects of professional development, according to HFRP, is that it must be customized, interactive, and provide real-life applicable strategies (Lopez & Patton, 2013). Traditional approaches to education, being lecture based, don't work if educators don't have a safe and supportive environment to try new strategies.

One of the newest approaches to come out is a blended learning model. This takes into account the fact that educators need to have time to brainstorm and problem solve in classroom-based and online methods in order to effectively apply strategies to multiple families. HFRP does have an electronic module that they have recently begun sharing that includes working through the evaluation of family dynamics and needs with reflection questions. This, coupled with instruction on best practices for communicating, resolving conflicts, and strengthening relationships, gives educators theory and practice to sharpen skills (Lopez & Patton, 2013).

PARENT MENTOR PROGRAMS

Did you know that parents are more likely to volunteer or engage in school-related activities when invited or encouraged to do so by other parents? This is the reason why a parent mentorship program can be so effective. There is this perception that to be a parent you must be all knowing. Yes, there is a certain degree of expertise that comes from raising your children, and gaining knowledge through reading and research is also possible, but expecting that all parents know *how* to be engaged is one of the biggest mistakes that a school can make.

Believe it or not, I am not a card-carrying member of my children's school PTO. Don't gasp, hear me out. I have been a PTO officer in the past and have readily spent hours packaging fundraisers and sending correspondence to parents, but at this point in my life that is not where I choose to spend my time. I do, however, consider myself to be one of those great volunteers who can show up with or without the meeting and fit right into whatever role I am assigned. Everyone is not comfortable doing this. Some well-meaning, committed parents are turned off by either over-zealous parents who make it seem like you have to live at the school, or dismissive ones who ignore the fact that you don't know where the adult-size restrooms are in the building. Without expecting parents to take a six-week course in parent volunteerism, a good parent engagement program will give ALL parents an overview of things that they need to know in order to be really helpful in or out of the building. Doing this efficiently is a challenge. A parent mentor program is a great way to do this.

Establish a pool of parents who are comfortable with the process and allow them to be a shoulder for support with new or less experienced parents. Offer once-a-month lunch or dinner options for parents to get engaged and connect mentors with mentees. These connections build community and offer parents a safe space to ask questions without feeling like they are wearing the newbie hat.

Knowing who should be your mentor is important. These parents need to be knowledgeable without being condescending. They have to be self-starters without being so chipper that they make everyone want to take a nap. I recommend having parents sign up for the mentor role a year at a time. This year's mentees are requested to be mentors the following year so that the pool is always replenished. The training program doesn't have to be overly formal, but content is critical. Providing a template for parents to use when "training" new parents can help. Here is a brief list of things to consider; there may be others that are specific to your school setting:

- Names of office staff
- Location of teacher rooms
- Location of restrooms
- District policies for volunteering
- Communication tips
- Confidentiality rules about being in the building
- Basic conflict resolution techniques

There are two versions of this that I think give us a great example of what success can look like. One is the parent mentor programs designed to guide parents through the world of special education. The Georgia Parent Mentor Partners program, which is similar to several others across the country, focuses on pairing parents of newly diagnosed students with parents who are comfortable with the process of special education and all that having a student with disabilities can entail. The training for this program allows the mentors to be jointly sponsored by the Georgia State Board of Education and the local districts with which they are partnered (Logan Square Neighborhood Association, 2015). In my state, a similar program is staffed by volunteer advocates. The goals of the programs are to support children by supporting the adults who care for them.

The other version is one that I became aware of through the Logan Square Neighborhood Association. Their parent mentor program is more in-line with training parents to be more active participants in the classroom (Georgia Parent Mentor Partnership, 2015). Their training, which includes content on classroom practices, prepares them to assist in the building by partnering with a teacher who is not their own child's teacher. They help to provide anything from reading support to an extra set of hands to teachers. In this program, stipends are provided for parents who meet a required amount of services, but similar programs exist around the country without payment. The goal is to empower parents as not only advocates and resources for their own children but for all children in the building. It has wonderful implications beyond giving jobs to parents. Growing up, the lunch lady was always someone's mother or aunt. The custodian was someone's father or uncle. The sense of community was strong. Children are much more likely to be respectful when they know the people have a strong connection to their home.

There are other ways of creating similar programs to communicate necessary information to parents in a systematic way. Here are a few other ideas of ways to get the information delivered:

Create a video. Have one or two parents or staff members cover the information that we reviewed in the earlier section and record it to be played for parents. This can be on a running loop in the parent resource center, played at school events, or even shared via e-mail or social media, if so inclined.

Share in the parent or school handbook. This would not be my first option, as I generally prefer not to make reading a requirement for getting information, but it can be a helpful possibility in addition to others. Most of the information can be put together in written format and should include pictures as often as possible.

PARENT RESOURCE CENTER

Parent resource centers have become increasingly popular and much more user-friendly from when they were originally laid out as a part of Title I programs. Not only do they contain information about community resources and learning supports, in many schools they become almost mini-community centers as homes to things like clothing exchanges, food pantries, and computer labs.

Beginning a good parent resource center starts with space. I've seen centers that are literally glorified closets and others that look more like libraries. Having a space that is easily accessible to all parents makes your center more appealing. The goal of a parent resource center is to have parents be provided with a centralized location for things like educational classes and information and to gain access to support services.

Often, parent liaisons are housed in the parent resource centers. These staff members are school employees whose primary responsibility is to connect parents to the school, acting as a bridge between school and home. They typically have little to no academic duties since they are often not certified employees. Parent liaisons might also be called "home school advisors" or "parent educators." Within the framework of the building, they have no academic duties with students and have more flexibility with regard to the services with which they can support parents. When they are stationed in the parent resource center, they may provide training for parents, operate computer labs, or facilitate tutoring programs by coordinating more effectively with community-based organizations. The "if you build it they will come" motto does not necessarily apply to anything in the school, and the parent resource center is no different. You will need to spend time making sure that the parents actually know about the resource and are encouraged to participate. One way to do that is to partner with teachers and have them include the parent center in their communications with families and also incorporate resources as recommendations. Creating incentives that might encourage use is another option.

> *Tip:* What is included in a parent resource center can vary wildly from school to school. You'll want to consider throughout the planning process what you actually hope to accomplish. Do you have a strong desire to increase literacy? You should have tools and potentially workshops presented that will support that. Are you struggling with parents helping with homework? You might need to include evening office hours to help parents gain those skills or partner with tutoring services to be offered through the center.

INTENTIONAL INCENTIVES:
INCENTIVES THAT REMOVE BARRIERS

Encouraging participation with incentives is a slightly controversial topic. Many in education philosophically disagree with "paying" parents to engage in their kids' education. But let's go back to our vision. Our goal is to create the conditions for parents to rise; that means we have to remove obstacles and barriers that may prevent or hinder parents from participating. For that reason, providing incentives that both encourage parents to participate and eliminate barriers can be an excellent addition to your engagement program. Some parents are on the fence about participating; others want to, but doing so puts them in a position of missing out on work or requiring child care that they don't have. I remember considering a co-op preschool when I was completing my graduate studies. I knew that the cost savings from this school choice would help me and I wasn't at all opposed to helping in the classroom either. They, however, required that I not bring my younger child with me when I volunteered. That meant I either needed to pay for child care or trust another parent to keep her when I was in the room. I didn't like either option, so I opted for a more traditional preschool. Had they allowed me to bring my child, or even offered a reasonably priced drop-in service, I may have chosen otherwise. This can very often be the case in elementary schools, where parents with younger children feel reluctant to bring the second and/or subsequent children into the building if they were to volunteer. Creating incentives that address the needs of your families is a win-win.

Many schools are prevented from spending school funds on purchasing gift cards, however, requesting gift card donations is a great way around that challenge. When parents have to choose between gas for work and gas for a parent conference, you can imagine which will fall off the list. If you provide gas cards for attendance, you create a situation where parents now have to talk themselves out of coming rather than talking themselves into it. Below is a list of other potential incentives that can be gained through donation or contract to support family engagement in your school. As always, this is not an all-inclusive list but is merely designed to help spark your own creativity. Remember to consider the types of families in your school, their needs, their wants, and also things that they may be hoping to avoid as a means of adding to this list:

- Gas cards
- Groceries
- Grocery cards
- Free admittance to school events

- Free childcare
- Family meals
- Transportation

Bonus Tip: This is another great option for parents who are not able or willing to be in the building. Perhaps you have a parent who is a daycare provider; partner with them to offer free or low-cost child care for events or during the day for parents who wish to come in and volunteer. They don't have to miss out on the job that provides for their family and they are still able to contribute to the needs of the school.

EDUCATOR INCENTIVES

As I write this book, there is an educator shortage in the state of Indiana. I suspect, without a great deal of research, that other areas of the country have similar shortages. The average educator entering the field, particularly those working in urban or high-needs districts, is expected to remain in the field for five years or less. As teachers retire, they are not being replaced at an equal rate, which combines with decreasing budgets to leave overworked teachers in front of overcrowded classrooms. Ultimately, for many, the demands are too high and the perks are so far and few between that they would rather leave the classroom in search of greater gains. During a recent institute focused on the intentional recruiting and retaining of quality equity-minded educators, the topic of teacher attrition was discussed. During this session, the focus was on educator pay and benefits, but the data were clear that more times than not, the real indication for improved teacher retention was related to school culture and climate. It is true that educators want and need more pay for the job that they do, but even when pay is equitable, teachers will leave the schools, and even the profession, when they don't feel well supported (Great Lakes Equity Center, 2015). The benefit to educational leaders is that, oftentimes, changes to school climate only require minor reallocation of resources rather than creation.

Another idea is rewarding educators in time. Most business professionals will tell you that time is our most limited resource. Regardless of income or status, we each have the same 24 hours in any day. Providing teachers with "comp" time, meaning that they can leave early or come in late to offset the hours that they give above and beyond the call of duty, can be very effective at preventing teacher burnout. Below is a list of other items I have seen work very well:

- Gift cards (donated)
- In-house spa day
- Staff lunch events
- Dress-down days

PARENT NIGHTS

With the help of the national parent and teacher organizations, parent nights have become a common line item on the school calendar. Most schools, particularly elementary, have several of these per year: one for literacy, one for math, one for science, and on and on. At the middle and high school levels, themes might include college and career readiness or social topics like bullying prevention and awareness. The goal is to bring parents to the building, provide them some content and instruction, and then hope that they will model and/or reinforce the concepts once they get home.

While many of these events do, in fact, succeed in bringing parents into the building, rarely can we say that they are successful. Why? Because we have no data to back up that statement. The randomness of the events doesn't allow us to definitively say we created something that provided parents with tools that they needed or even that the students or staff benefited long term from what was presented. Generally sponsored at least in part by the parent and teacher organization, many times the events occur with too few volunteers, and although the concept is good, something is lost in translation as extra people in small spaces leaves much to be desired. When done well, these events fit into a more formalized plan. For example, let's take math night. If we plan math night at the beginning of a certain math unit and ask teachers to make the homework associated with the event, you are more likely to be able to gauge whether or not the event was a success. Anyone who completed the event homework attended and anyone who did not, well they didn't. Over the course of the unit, you can determine which group was more successful and know that what was presented impacted the outcome.

Another idea uses social media, which is one of my favorite tools for engaging families. Ask every parent to check in electronically on one or more social medial platforms and run surveys regarding the event, asking for future volunteer commitments and the like. This doesn't give you data regarding academics, per se, but it does allow you to see which of your families are willing to communicate with you in that way. This is helpful for future events. Ask parents what they need help with and they are more inclined to attend events. Perhaps you focused on math, but they want help with literacy. Possibly you planned an evening event and they would prefer one during the day. Data help us make decisions that are justifiable and relevant. Make sure all of your events are linked to data.

TAKE-HOME FAMILY ACTIVITY PACKS

In 1946, when the first drive-through restaurant was invented, it was probably a crazy concept to think that families would happily take a bag of food from a window and, dare we think of it, eat food without the benefit of the family table, plates, napkins, and all the items that are traditionally a part of mealtime. The American culture at that time dictated a standard routine related to meals, and, as such, most restaurateurs aligned themselves with those standards. But low and behold, fast forward to 2015 and you can barely pass a corner without seeing multiple drive-through windows. Why is that? The times have changed. Family structures and dynamics have changed dramatically over the past 20–30 years, but most of what we continue to do in family engagement practices still mirrors what we began doing decades ago.

Parent events, as we discussed in the previous section, are designed to model for parents the concepts and tools that we hope that they will use at home. The goal is often to build comfort levels in parents and teach skills that can be used to reinforce content delivery from the classroom. We also learned why sometimes these events are not as effective as we would hope. They sometimes fail because the parents who we really want to attend might not and the ones who do attend might have been successful whether they attended or not. Add to this the fact that the same exhausted teachers who spend their time in the classroom are the ones at the event until 8 p.m. and are the same ones who have to be back for morning duty at 7 a.m.

ANATOMY OF STRONG FAMILY EVENTS

Event planning has become a multi-million dollar industry in this country, from perfectly paired napkins and tablecloths to themed events and costumes. The successful execution of a family event at a school requires many of the same preparation steps. However, it typically has none of the budget but the added pressure of meeting the expectation of all types of families and delivering content that can be used to support student development.

Most school-sponsored events for families are either organized by school staff for the presentation to families or by a select group of families for the entire student body. In either event, the following planning notes can help take your event from an unstructured or ineffective mess to more enjoyable and successful. The goal of building community and skills is a lofty one but can be accomplished by following a few guidelines.

Pre-Event Strategy

Early in the school year or during the previous end-of-year planning sessions, create a framework for the school year activity. A sequential or logical flow to the events helps build upon consistent themes. For instance, if your school has a different character or academic theme of the month, your events should mirror the content that is being presented during the year. Different states promote college awareness throughout the school year, and many schools have college and career resources available to students during the school day. Opening the school during this time to share the content with families is a natural theme for an event. Some high schools have financial aid preparation events, so what about including colleges with adult programs as well? Elementary and middle schools can partner with high schools to promote at the lower levels and share resources such as volunteers and funds for giveaways and meals. Stretching budgets is a common concern among both small and large districts, and overwhelming volunteers is something that all schools should consider. Also, keeping parents from having to attend multiple events with multiple children makes it more likely that you can increase attendance.

Coordination

A truly effective family event should rarely be planned by one person. A collaborative effort generally elicits the most successful events. I recommend creating a team or committee, including members of multiple grade levels, parents, and even some students. This will allow for multiple perspectives that create events to appeal to more families. To ensure that no one person has to take on too much of the burden, you can rotate leadership of the event or assign leadership to the parent liaison or outreach specialist as one of their job duties.

Event Schedule

Pre-Event Activities

Not all families will arrive at the events at the same time. Some will arrive with time to spare and others will be running through at the last minute. One of the most important things you can do is have proper organization, which allows families to easily get directions for participating in the event as well as things to do while waiting. Last school year, one of my children's schools hosted a family fun fair. The event was basically an end-of-year activity with no real content delivery, just fun. Not a problem, but not as effective as it could be. However, they requested volunteers and even offered families who volunteered extra benefits such as free activities at the event. Great perk! Unfortunately, volunteers had very little information and the sheets that parents were given to explain the event were complicated, meaning that the volunteers had difficulty explaining everything to families when they came to purchase wristbands and tickets. This made for a huge bottleneck right at the front door. As parents came in, they were confused. Those who were there for only the classroom presentation of the event didn't know whether they were expected to pay or not, and since many hadn't gotten the full run-down of events, they were unprepared. In years past, unbeknownst to me, there had been credit and debit cards accepted; this year was cash only, so you can only imagine how that went over. All in all, most families did have a good time, but the event made for some pretty hectic moments and frustrated individuals as well.

Event Activities

The structure and flow of the main event is also important to your overall effectiveness. Having sufficient space, instructions, and assistance can take a good event and either put it over the top or tank the best intentions. I'll use an example of a school literacy event that was planned recently at one of the schools with which I work. Based around the book fair, one staff member was planning an activity that was to show early literacy skills using rhyming words. Simple enough. But since most of the families in this school speak Spanish, some only Spanish, we had to account for the fact that they may not know the English word for the pictures that they were trying to rhyme. Our solution was to put a word bank with each matching game. Then we thought about the fact that many of them don't read English either, so the solution for that was having a volunteer at the table to assist with instructions. This was a lot to consider and only one piece of the overall event, but it's the kind of thing that has to be considered when planning an event.

Wrap-Up/Closing

After the event activities are complete, it can be nice to have the families take something with them. Anything from a tip sheet showing how to apply the newly acquired skills to a home-based activity that may reinforce the skills. Adding this is that little touch that can expand the benefit of the event long beyond the one day.

Like everything we've discussed in this book, the goal is not only the quality of the èvents we host but also the outcomes. The best-laid intentions that are unsuccessful have done nothing to improve the relationships between the parents and the schools. Using Figure 5.4, the Event Planning Guide, as a template, review your most recent or next

Figure 5.4 Event Planning Guide

Pre-Event

Venue: _____

Date/Time: _____ Confirmed by _____

Coordinator/Team Leader: _____

Volunteers Needed:

- Prep/Shopping _____
- Setup _____
- Greeters _____
- Floaters _____
- Main event(s) _____
- Tear-down/Cleanup _____

Budget: Total _____

Volunteer Perks: _____

Materials: _____

Space/Tool/Equipment Rental: _____

Food: _____

Staff/Personnel: _____

Event Details

Theme/Goals: _____

Room/Event Setup: _____

Activities:

Pre-session activities/Welcome: _____

Main event(s): _____

Closing: _____

Follow-up/Take-home packets: _____

Cleanup/Tear-down

anticipated event for organization. You can add names of people who are in charge of certain areas and also add budget totals to the sheet to document the financial plan. Another option is to include ways to continue the conversation. Will teachers give posttests to students? Or will standardized test scores be your tracking point? Yes, you can have events just for fun, but with schools competing against so many other activities that take up those coveted after-school hours, you also want to get the best bang for your buck.

Post-Event Data Collection (If Needed)

In-school events can be a good part of your overall plan if they are planned well and not overutilized. An alternative that I've found to be effective, both in cost and time, is the take-home event pack. It started as a twist on a traditional school/family dinner. Having partnered with a local Fraternal Order of Police (FOP) lodge to offer every family in our building a free Thanksgiving-style dinner in the fall, we knew that it was a popular and pleasant way to have both community engagement and share the benefits of family mealtime. In the spring, there was less interest in a marathon meal prep and delivery event but still a desire to have a similar connection to families. We were fortunate to receive a generous donation from Hurst Bean Company, which provided us with over 200 bags of ready-to-cook beans and seasoning packets. Those alone would have been a wonderful meal for a small family or, with minor additions, could stretch and supply extended family as well. With the beans, we sent home notes about the importance of family mealtime, conversation starters, and preparation suggestions. Providing the material in English and Spanish and sending them home in the backpacks of every student removed some of the traditional barriers to family events.

As a twist, I asked families to share photos of their mealtimes with the school. This was less successful than originally hoped for, but I did hear from several families that they enjoyed the meal and the activities that came with them. In the future, I plan to use a hashtag or offer a prize for families who share; this way it will be more of a conversation. Several organizations offer premade templates and packages for these types of events.

Similar events that can be done in a take-home format are listed below. Do you have other ideas that you have or plan to implement? Share them with me on Twitter, Facebook, or Pinterest @indyparentcoach.

Math Night	Provide families with flash cards, either made by children in school and laminated or purchased, along with a set of game ideas to reinforce math concepts.
Science Night	Provide the family with a recipe and coupons, if available, for a cooking challenge, with reflection questions to reinforce science concepts.
Literacy Night	Create a hashtag such as #Enlacereads and ask families to tweet you their favorite books from bedtime stories. Add book titles to a bulletin board for families not engaged in social media.
Health and Wellness Night	Choose a healthy habit to reinforce for the school, such as sleep. Provide families with educational material to teach the habit. Create a chart to monitor the families' progress as they implement the skill and allow students to turn in the chart and get their names on a bulletin board, showing how families are putting the info to good use.
Services Learning Night	Have families share in a service learning initiative. Provide a baggie of card-making items and ask families to return one card to share with local hospitals or nursing homes.

PARENT OPEN HOUSE OR OPEN DOOR HOURS

Many educators complain about low attendance to parent-teacher conference times. Working in schools, I know that 10–20 percent attendance is typical and rarely includes the families that you "need" to see. Conference times can be extremely stressful for all parties involved, particularly because they are typically linked to grades and/or performance. However, having parents and teachers face-to-face is a win-win, as it gives transparency that is essential.

An alternative that has been implemented in some schools is open door hours. I started seeing these in private schools in my area where they were hoping to give prospective parents a feel for the real-time experience that the school provided. Once per week, there are open house hours. Typically, there is a staff member present to provide prospective families with a tour, but the twist that we provide in our school is that we also allow this to be a time when current families can expect quick access to staff members as well. We have time each week and ask families from our PTO to help man the ship. We invite parents to sit in class and partake of our unique school model. It's a great way for the feeling of community to be shared with current and prospective families, and there is very little cost associated with these types of events.

FUNDING YOUR PARENT ENGAGEMENT PROGRAM

The first place you look for engagement funds is the Title I budget. But in most schools these funds cover interventionists, academic resources, and other items that don't traditionally fit into the school line-item budget. Getting administrators on board to contribute a portion of this money to engagement can be easier said than done, and most often what they are willing to spend the funds on is program curriculum material.

In a perfect world, you will not need to create a budget for your program, but in the real world, where schools are struggling more than ever to maintain necessary academic components of the school plan, there may be very little left to be directed to parent engagement efforts. In the budget area of the plan, you'll want to consider the following items and address them in some way. This is one of those non-all-inclusive lists again, as your specific situation will depend, at least in part, on the families that you serve. This is a good starting point, but refer to the parent empathy maps when considering additional costs you may want to include. For example, in one area, you may have to offer incentives of gas cards or bus passes, since parents may not be able to make it to the school without these services. In other areas, this might not be necessary at all.

BACKGROUND CHECKS

In my area, it is not uncommon for districts to charge new employees or volunteers for background checks. I firmly believe that these are critical in ensuring that we are protecting our children. However, if I, as a parent, know that I will not be able to pass a background check, how exactly does this make me feel? Perhaps I can pass it, but if the $30 fee is cost prohibitive for me, am I supposed to announce my poverty to the front office staff? Access to public resources can sometimes cause us to forget that for many families there is shame associated with their inability to provide for their families—just like the student who would rather be labeled as defiant and take a zero rather than acknowledge they don't understand the homework assignment. Considering several options for families who either choose not to or are unable to pass the background check shows that all families are welcome to participate in the school.

Some ideas for parents who don't need to pass a background check include the following:

- Prepping classroom materials at home
- Soliciting donations
- Reading at home

- Preparing materials at home
- Coordinating out-of-school, parent-only events

I suggest having this information on the back of the background check form. Train staff to present the form front and back to parents, stating something to the effect of, "Here is our form for background checks. If you plan to volunteer in our building, you will need complete this form and turn it in. If you prefer to help outside of the building, the background check may not be necessary and you can perform these tasks in support of the school as well."

You can also look at alternative sources of payment for these background checks or offer scholarship funds to families by checking that they cannot afford the fee. Soliciting donations from local businesses for the fund can show that they are willing to support safe schools, and acknowledging the sponsorship can be an advertisement for them as well. Many schools offset the cost by having more limited criminal record checks. Those decisions are generally more related to district demographics. In general, quality reports are worth the cost, but they should not be a hindrance to families who are committed to engaging.

SUPPLIES/MATERIALS

The number of supplies you procure for your activities will depend upon which programming you choose to include. Many schools that plan to offer parent workshops, for instance, will purchase ready-made curriculum. The cost for this can range from a few hundred to several thousand dollars. In almost every instance, there will also be consumable costs. Things like paper, pencils, crafting supplies, and even food will fall under this category. On page 93, there is a parent event planning page. Working through this will help you consider the variety of costs that you may run into with your events.

It's not uncommon that purchasing supplies eats up a considerable amount of the budget. One way to prevent this is to ask parents to either provide or request donations as a part of the plan. With a little planning, you can know well enough in advance of the event to request the supplies you need ahead of time. Often, families are happy to clean out the garage and provide their unneeded items to the school for the benefit of the program.

VOLUNTEER TRAINING AND ACKNOWLEDGMENT

We already talked about the parent mentoring program and how it can help other parents learn all that is necessary when working in the building.

However, in many states now, bullying prevention training is required for all school staff, students, parents, and volunteers. With limited knowledge of best practices in these areas, it is possible that you will need to provide additional training beyond the basic level to ensure that parents and volunteers are well versed in recognizing and preventing bullying in the school.

RECOGNITION AND REWARDS

The National PTO does an excellent job of encouraging recognition of parent volunteers. Because this is a parent-led organization, the recognition generally comes from other parents. I recommend that schools, as a part of the parent engagement program, incorporate recognition of parents who are supporting the children and/or the school. Take into consideration that many of our parents today had difficult educational experiences. I can't tell you the number of times that I have a student who struggles academically or socially and the parents tell me their own story of poor progress. We already talked about the emotional responses that can prevent parents from being proactive in education. Remember, we are trying to take away every potential negative that is blocking them from engaging and add anything that we can to make it more appealing. If you have a parent who was never successful in school, their name on a bulletin board costs you nothing but can mean the world to them and their student.

With a little help from the site www.ptotoday.com, here are a few more ideas about how schools can reach out to show appreciation for parents:

Thank-You Notes. A good friend of mine could single-handedly keep the Hallmark Store in business. I, on the other hand, never grew up giving or receiving cards other than birthdays. With the normalcy of electronic communication, the nostalgia and novelty of a simple thank-you note can go quite a long way.

Feature in Newsletter. If your school has a regularly produced weekly or monthly newsletter, spend a few minutes highlighting a family from your building. It can be someone who volunteers in the building or even someone who just does a great job at home. As parents see other parents doing things, the idea that these tasks are doable becomes less overwhelming.

Reserved Parking Space. I know there are many times when I attend school events and I am searching for a parking place. What about designating a parking space for the volunteer of the month? The cost is minimal and the winner can be recognized on a bulletin board where they share their favorite ways to fit in volunteer hours.

Announcement. When you know that you will have volunteers in the building, have the principal, or whoever makes morning announcements, remind everyone to stop in and say hello and thanks to the volunteer of the day.

Vision

- There are so many program components to choose from. Which components do you currently have in your program?
- Which components would you like to add?
- Do you have any program components that are less effective or more costly, in time or resources, than others?
- Eliminating activities that are not effective is a great place to start. Assess all current activities financially first—do they bring in a profit or break even? Then assess in terms of cost of resources, such as volunteer hours; finally, consider the benefit. Rank activities in order from least expensive to most and most expensive to least; ideally there should be some clear winners and losers.

Plan

- When will you hold activities?
- Scheduling your program components in an orderly fashion allows you to let each build upon the previous. As you accomplish this, you minimize planning and maximize effectiveness by eliminating duplication.

Action

- Do you need to secure financial information from other sources?
- Are there other data points you would like to consider for effectiveness? Test scores, attendance, and behavioral referrals are all good ideas.

(Continued)

(Continued)

Notes/Brainstorming

Expanding the Tools in Your Toolbox

6

We become what we behold. We shape our tools, and thereafter our tools shape us.

—Marshall McLuhan

When I started writing this book, my hope was that I would encourage others to expand both their idea of what engaged parents looked like and that they would feel more capable and committed to engaging all parents. By adding what I call the lens of engagement, we go from haphazard activities to inclusionary practices. Part of what I know is that the tools we have at our disposal are not always perfectly aligned with the goals that we have for our students and families. There will be times when we need to pull out different tools or sharpen ones at which we've already become skilled. In this chapter, we'll talk about some of the less obvious strategies that I have found to be helpful along the way.

MOTIVATIONAL INTERVIEWING

The concept of motivational interviewing is one that was designed to work with patients who have a substance abuse history and are reluctant to seek treatment for their addiction. Most individuals who are addicts have some awareness that their addictions are, in fact, causing problems in their lives. They can acknowledge that there are things which could be better should they opt to enter treatment, but there are generally both physiological and emotional attachments that cause the patient to be in a state of ambivalence about choosing to forgo the substance. Motivational interviewing helps the patient see the benefits of entering treatment by gradually building discrepancies between the life that they state they want and the life that they currently have (Relias Learning, 2014). The illumination of barriers and identification of solutions makes this more effective.

In working with parents who are reluctant to engage with their children's education, looking at current and previously gathered data, most often parents can see some benefit in their role as support for the child. However, their reluctance may not signal disinterest as much as it signals the need for support. Think of it as a path. To engage reluctant parents, we are seeking to shine a light on an unseen path, removing stones and debris that might trip them up.

While being a master at motivational interviewing is not likely to occur without additional supports and training, these techniques can be used in variations during conferences, in e-mail correspondence, and even in phone calls. Here are the essential steps and how they can be applied to reluctant parents:

1. *Establish rapport.* Make your first contact a positive one, seeking first to understand and then to be understood. If the ideal scenario is that parents and teachers are partners, start early and often at establishing this relationship. Things like positive phone calls, notes home, and activity on social media all allow for emotional or psychological connection to be created. This can be done from day one before any problems occur. If you have not done that yet, or worse yet, the problems started from your earliest meetings, this can still be accomplished. Without sounding salesy, begin your conversation with a positive like "Johnny is so much fun in class," or "Jada had a great day yesterday." When necessary, you can even choose to focus on a positive that you hope will occur, such as "We've just started this unit and I think Juan has plenty of time to grasp the material."

2. *Assess readiness.* Very often, particularly in the classroom, teachers assume parent ability and/or readiness as it relates to supporting students. I recall getting a homework assignment that was a "family project" to be completed over a period of time. It required tools that are not at all uncommon to the average American family, such as scissors, glue, crayons, and a hole punch. I remember thinking how unlikely it would be that many of my clients would have all of the necessary tools to complete this project, but there was not space to mention that on the packet that was to be

received back at the school a little over a week from the time it was given. Taking into account that not everyone is always as ready as we would like gives us a chance to meet people where they are rather than leaving gaps, which can lead to miscommunications or conflict.

3. *Assess motivation and confidence.* It is possible for a parent to be ready to work but lack motivation and confidence in the skills that they need. Recall our survey results, where parents have consistently stated that they value homework yet feel less capable to assist with it than they would like. This can lead to decreases in motivation or lack of confidence. Think of something that you are not successful or talented at doing, maybe singing if you are not musically inclined. What if I suggested that you try out for the last season of the singing competition *American Idol?* Even though you know you could get something out of the experience, you most likely will not have a great deal of confidence in your ability to win, so you'll be less motivated to attempt it. If, however, you're a talented musician, you might jump at the chance. Parents' lack of follow-through can be an indicator of skill but not always intention.

4. *Parent identifies problems and solutions.* This can be tricky, but this is critical. Parents who identify the problems and necessary solutions are more likely to follow through with solutions chosen. Take, for example, an IEP case conference; you know that the student needs an additional 30 minutes of reading nightly to support improvement in fluency. One way to do this is lay it out and tell the parents that they need to read nightly. Perhaps this will work, but maybe not. The other option is to provide a printout that shows the suggested amount of minutes per day that the student needs and let the parents come to the conclusion that they can give 10 minutes per day to the cause once they have seen the visual representation. Most adults like being in control of their own choices; that doesn't change just because you become a parent.

5. *Identify next actions and follow-up.* This could be as simple as establishing a progress monitoring system with accountability notes for all of the team. To ensure clarity, it's a good idea to give written plans and document the process of follow-up. When parents are in meetings, some have told me they feel overwhelmed by the amount of information that they receive. A written e-mail to follow up or a plan that can be copied and sent home helps to ensure that everyone is on the same page.

HOME VISITS

One of the most underutilized tools in successful parent engagement program is home visits. On a recent professional development (PD) session, I asked a room full of educators how many of them did home visits. Not one teacher raised his or her hand. The school counselor and the parent outreach coordinator both stated that they did do the visits, but none of the teachers had ever seen where their students lived. I went a little further and asked the teachers if there were any particular reasons why they chose not to do visits. I expected to hear things like "We don't have enough time," or even "I'm scared to go into these homes," but what I got was surprising to me.

"I feel like that would be imposing," said one teacher.

I had never thought of it that way. It made perfect sense that a teacher might feel like entering another person's home was a crossing of boundaries. But isn't that what teachers do all the time? We give students homework and class projects to complete at home. We are essentially entering the home and creating expectations with no invitation. What I want us to begin to think about is the idea that visiting homes will give us a greater view into the realities of our students. If done correctly, a good home visit can do the following:

- Help the staff gain valuable information about the student and family
- Strengthen the connection between the student and the staff member
- Preventively address potential problems through universal screening
- Allow for more informal communication about difficult topics
- Effectively increase academic outcomes
- Improve attendance

The Parent/Teacher Home Visit Project has been doing excellent research on the benefit of home visits on staff and students since 1998. It is designed on a model that teaches educators how to complete a two-visit plan: one in the fall focusing on relationship building and another that builds on skills such as academic supports that can be implemented in the home to support outcomes at school. They believe a two-visit model builds both relationships and skills (The Parent/Teacher Home Visit Project, 2011).

The project believes that the following five components make their program stand out compared to other models, which are more often concerned with addressing problematic behaviors in schools by meeting with parents to get information to support interventions in school:

- Families and teachers are equally important co-educators, given that the family is the expert on the individual child while the teacher is the expert on the curriculum that must be mastered for success.
- Before important information about academic status can be effectively shared, positive communication must be established and barriers addressed.
- All students and families should be visited because targeting challenging students will only perpetuate the cycles of mistrust.
- All families have the ability to assist their child in their academic success and that effective family involvement can happen in every home—in light of recent research conclusions on effective family engagement.
- This project should be voluntary for all involved and teachers should be compensated for their time (The Parent/Teacher Home Visit Project, 2011).

Whether your district uses the project or not, here are some helpful tips for making successful home visits:

When possible, make contact before your visit. When necessary, I have made uninvited visits to student homes; however, I don't advise you do this often or alone. Typically, this happens when there is an emergency or when we have been unable to make contact with the parents for some other reason. Arriving at a home uninvited is intrusive. It is necessary at times, but it can set the family up to be defensive and that's never a good way to start the visit. The contact before should be honest and give the parents an idea of why you are coming. When I am going to do a home visit as a part of the special education testing process, sometimes I am going to get as much background information for the developmental history as possible. In that case, I let the parents know ahead of time that I will be bringing forms that I will help them complete as a part of the process.

Search for buried treasure. On a recent visit to a client home, I walked in and was surprised to see that they had moved three new family members into the home. As such, the house was overcrowded with toys and laundry and was not what I would have considered to be in good, clean condition. When I met with my client, she told me how she actually appreciated the extra hands in the home because they made it easier for her to care for her two young children and newborn. What I realized is how easy it is to miss little positive notes when the challenges or inconveniences are so large. Is the home warm? Do they have adequate food? Do the children appear happy? Did the family welcome you to a meal? All of these are things you could miss if you were only focused on delivering a form or securing commitment for a school-based meeting. Be intentional as you seek positives in the family home; it cuts down on our natural tendency to be judgmental.

Be prepared. When I make a home visit, I keep a folding chair in my trunk, Febreeze in the glove box, leave my purse and any valuables in the car, and keep my cell phone handy. In my portfolio, I typically keep things like a list of area food pantries and other resources that might come up during the course of our conversation. On occasion, I will use my phone to Google a resource for a family, but having paper copies helps so that you don't have to rely on a signal and it cuts down on time that can be spent communicating.

Expect the unexpected. The conditions of the average middle-class home compared to an inner-city urban or even rural home can be completely opposite. Ruby Payne's work on poverty was quite controversial in the generalizations that she made about family life and home conditions in many impoverished homes, but in reality, many of her assertions were correct. There is often excessive background noise in the home, which can be off-putting to staff who are attempting to have a conversation over the television or radio. It is not unreasonable to ask a parent to adjust the conditions to make for a more effective visit, but do understand that you are in their home and such requests can be seen as judgmental. Choose your comments wisely and make them in the most pleasant tone to avoid triggering a defense mechanism in parents.

Think outside of the home. This may sound counterproductive, but if the family home is something you are not completely comfortable with or you are not welcome in the home, consider having your "home visit" in the community. Many areas have a community center, church, or park that is easily accessible, close to home, and a perfectly neutral place to have a brief meeting. Asking a parent if you can meet them at the park can also give you a chance to speak without the concern of younger children in and out of the conversation while you are trying to make a connection with the parent.

Be a supermodel. The home visit is the perfect time to casually model appropriate behaviors or interactions or reinforce recently learned skills.

If you are able, take materials to your visit that you can use to teach a particular topic. For example, perhaps you have a couple of students who are struggling with reading; take a book from your personal library and lend it to the student by starting the story and then having them finish it with you. Ask the student to please return the book to you the following day, and you've just added on a lesson in responsibility.

Leave a parting gift or follow up with a card. In my younger days I never would have considered this, but I have become a big fan of personal touches now, so I also suggest following up with a thank-you card. This lets the parent know that you appreciate their time and it makes sure that the visitors wrap up the visit with a positive.

Now we're going to look at a couple of common concerns that I would be remiss not to mention.

Safety should be a focus. Although extremely rare, there have been reports of injury and even death related to social workers or child welfare agency workers while engaging in home visit-type events. The reality is that many of the families you want to help are living under dire circumstances, which can make them willing to do things that are unethical or illegal. Being careful is a practical and reasonable thing to do. Go during daylight hours, make sure your staff is aware when you are going, and if you become uncomfortable with the situation, leave politely and don't second guess your decision.

Schedules may be a concern. The Parent/Teacher Home Visit Project is very clear that teachers should be compensated for their time, but many schools struggle with how to effectively manage this and not be short staffed in the classroom. I recommend providing substitute teachers on a rotating basis to allow teachers at least one day per month for visits. This may not allow for students to be present during the visit, which is a concern as well, but it does eliminate the need for teachers to use weekend hours. Another option is to schedule additional in-service days on the school calendar. This pay is built into the teacher salary, and because students are not in class, parents are more likely to be home. For an average class of 25 students, providing that most families live within a reasonable distance of each other, quarterly in-service days would accommodate at least one visit per home. For middle and high school teachers, more days may be needed. Another option would be weekend visits; teachers should be compensated with their choice of overtime pay or comp time for the hours worked.

Teachers may not be prepared. Because most educators have never been trained on completing a home visit, there will likely be some initial hesitation or discomfort in scheduling and completing these visits. Staff training is essential to both safety and effectiveness. I lean toward making these mandatory, particularly during the primary grades when the establishment of a strong school and home partnership can be cultivated more easily. With that being said, however, resistant and reluctant teachers, especially when untrained, can be either ineffective or counterproductive to the ultimate goal. Typically, resistance comes from either teachers who are uncomfortable with the process or those who feel overwhelmed by other responsibilities. Teacher pre-surveys can be helpful in addressing those concerns.

Funding. Compensation for teacher time, reimbursement for travel expenses, and material to be presented at home visits does not come for free. However, some schools have found enough funds to cover the programming through federal and private grant sources.

Be very clear that the homes you enter may be completely different from anything you've ever experienced. I recall going into one home and there being no chairs. None. There was a couch in the front room and beds in both bedrooms but no actual chairs. My client at that time offered me a seat on her bed, after she brushed some clothes off of it, and really thought nothing of it. I've been in other homes that were historic and beautiful, warm and inviting. The truth is, you never know what you will come across when you enter someone else's home, and the thought of even asking to enter can feel like an intrusion. There will be parents who will not allow you to enter their home. I have had parents meet me on the porch and have a full conversation without inviting me in. The connection can still be made, right there on the stoop, if you handle things well.

When it works, it works well. A school in Indiana, New Market Elementary School, combined academic standards with the home visit model. Teacher Susan McVay used lessons about maps to have her students create their own maps showing the way from the school to their homes. Imagine the pride in the eyes of the student and the family in this situation. Imagine if a problem did come up, how much less likely a parent would be to blame the teacher who she saw follow her child's drawing directly to her home. These kinds of connections are possible in other ways, but home visits are a logical place to begin. For a letter to introduce the visits to your families, see the following box.

Dear parents,

This year, _____ (school) has a goal of building a stronger community by connecting individually with each family in the home.

The purpose of these visits is to

- Strengthen teacher and family relationships
- Model the partnership between the school and the family for your child
- Expand the community atmosphere by reaching outside of our walls

During our visit, which can take place in your home or Neighborhood Park or community center of your choice, your child and any other family members who you would like us to meet are welcome to attend. We will ask you some questions about your child and family and be able to answer questions for you as well. Some of our families will be highlighted in the school newsletter and bulletin board from time to time.

Studies show that these types of programs have increased student academic achievement and improved parent engagement in schools. It has brought teachers and families closer together and created opportunities for better communications between home and school, all of which we love.

Over the course of the school year, your child's teacher will contact you to schedule a home visit. Our school social worker or administrators may ask to attend as well. You are also welcome to request the visit if you have a date or time that you know will work well for your family. This is NOT a meeting to tell you what to do as a parent. This is a time to get to know you and your student away from school. This is also a time for you to get to know your student's teacher.

We look forward to meeting with you soon. Please do not hesitate to contact your child's teachers if you have questions or would like to schedule your visit.

Sincerely,
Mrs. Day
School Social Worker

POSITIVE REINFORCEMENT

We often discuss positive reinforcement when we talk about students with behavioral challenges, but engaging reluctant parents can also use a dose of positivity. We already talked about the fact that many parents have a negative view of education in general, and, for some, the perception is even more specific to a school or district and they are more or less waiting for the bad things to happen. Getting these parents to see that not only are good things happening in the school but that they can help even more great things happen will require the development of a relationship.

I want you to think about your first puppy-love affair. Without dating myself too terribly, did you pass notes? Hopefully at least a few of you remember those ornately folded notes with "For your eyes only" scribbled across the front. Well even if you don't, just try and stay with me. Even today, in this technologically savvy world, a paper note or letter can be a remarkably refreshing change of pace. For parents who are used to receiving negative notes, poor report cards, or bills from the school, a handwritten note thanking them for helping with a project or personally inviting them to an event is a welcomed change. This is helpful for reluctant parents, but it doesn't hurt to use it with all your parents. Make a habit of working your way through your class list once a month.

ENGAGING RELUCTANT PARENTS/CAREGIVERS

Throughout this book, I have provided you with a number of tools, strategies, and ideas for engaging all families. I hope that it helps you be more intentional with your efforts. It's important to note that we also need to be realistic. The perception that any set of tools will be 100 percent effective in engaging all families is a fallacy that I do not want to claim. Our goal is always to remove as many barriers as possible in an effort to make the probability of success greater. In some instances we cannot, either for lack of tools or resources, truly remove the barriers blocking the parents' engagement in their students' education. I believe those instances are few and far between as we move toward improving tools for all educators. However, even in instances when the needs are beyond the scope of what we can realistically provide, the effort that can be devoted toward change can still have a lasting impact if educators approach the situation with the best possible frame of mind. As we talk about reluctant parents or those with circumstances blocking engagement, understand that your thoughts are powerful forces that give direction to your speech and actions. Both of those can make or break the relationships you are working to build.

We've already established the value in parents and families being supportive in education, but before we talk about the situations that really can cause significant disconnection between school and home, I want to take a brief walk down memory lane as it relates to the traditional educational model that most of us in the United States would assume is "normal."

The modern education system that we know today, namely free, accessible public education for all, has not always been viewed by the general public in the same way. This version became commonplace from the late nineteenth century into the early twentieth century. I have to note that at its earliest stages, it wasn't truly accessible to all, and what was available to some was not an adequate comparison to what was available to others. However, from the earliest foundation, one of the main purposes of the system was to prepare children, both American citizens and immigrants, to be the most productive members of society that they could be. With the transition to a more industrialized nation, the goal became to prepare children to be competitive in the global economy. Textbooks were invented to essentially create a template for all educators to provide a universal method of providing content to all students. During this time, teachers were considered to be experts, and parents were not necessarily looked at to provide instruction or intervention in the academic setting. Parents were to support the authority of the teacher by providing structure and discipline for children. Teachers were revered in the community and their position was as respected as they were as individuals.

Even in the twentieth century, when most of our current educators were born and raised, there was still a more classic delineation between what the school was to do and what the home was to do. I saw a commercial recently that talked about playing. The premise was related to how common it was for children in the 1980s and 1990s to go out to play with friends after homework time and be gone until almost bedtime, coming home only for dinner if they hadn't had it before they went out. The expectation that homework was a long and drawn-out group experience has really only become the norm in the past two decades.

Now, it is not only believed that parents should assist with homework completion, it is expected. And it's not just homework; enrichment, extracurricular, and volunteer duties have all made their way onto the to-do list of parents in the twenty-first century. The expectation is that parents are to be partners in education, working with children in collaboration with teachers to help students be productive members of society. The problem with this concept is that not all parents are as interested as others in being a part of this partnership, and not all have the skills that they need to be truly effective. For these reasons and many more, parents can be reluctant or even oppositional to engaging in education. Below are some additional reasons why parents might be disengaged, as well as some ideas for working through these challenges. You may have come across some of these considerations when you were completing the parent empathy map as well.

Limited Education

The graduation rates in this country over the last 30 years have increased some, but based upon the ages of the average parent now, we would need to look around the late 1980s and '90s to see how many people were graduating from high school successfully or moving on to college degrees. Because of this, many parents who are raising children now may feel academically incapable of supporting their children. In my workshops I often tell people, even with my master's degree, I still have trouble helping my children with their homework beyond third or fourth grade. I have a great deal of empathy for the many parents who have to adjust to Common Core and struggle in more ways than you can even imagine.

I generally remind current teachers that the educational reform that we are all so invested in now was in fact initiated due to the failed models that educated our current parents. Some of the schools which have now been "taken over" because of consistently failing to make adequate yearly progress were the alma maters of the parents who walk through your doors. While not every parent is ill-equipped to be academically invested in the lives of their child, you need to assume that in your classroom there is a spectrum of ability. That same spectrum is also going on in the home.

What You Can Do. Connect parents to tutoring programs for students. When I worked in a middle school, we had no budget for a tutoring program to be established and our request for local university students yielded no volunteers. However, we knew that we had several students who needed to have a safe, quiet, and orderly space to complete homework. Some of them occasionally needed a little help, but often it was just the consistency that was holding them back. We came up with a peer tutoring program that helped students and families. Older students helped younger students; parents only had to handle transportation.

Mental or Physical Illness

Are you familiar with Maslow's hierarchy of needs? Basic physical needs and safety are the base. Things like homework and science projects are not on the list. If you have families who are struggling with mental or physical illness, getting them to engage in volunteer duties will likely not occur, but that doesn't mean that they are uninterested or oblivious. They often have tough choices to make with their limited time and money, and most of what goes on in the school simply will not hold a candle to the higher-order needs.

What You Can Do. Connect families with community resources and engage families by offering support rather than asking. Mentoring programs are an amazing addition to the family constellation. For the student, they get the perk of having another adult, without higher needs, who can be a consistent part of their life; they can also help support the ailing parent and keep in communication with the school.

Financial Instability

We've talked about this several times, but poverty is an incredibly expensive lifestyle. The amount of time and energy required to maintain a family when you live below the poverty line is pretty unbelievable. Stop and think about what you would have to do without today if your income was minimum wage. Even if you live in a state where the minimum wage is higher than the federal requirement, it's likely that your families who are living this lifestyle make some tough choices when the end of the money comes before the end of the week.

What You Can Do. Ensure that all projects you want completed at home come home with all the necessary tools. Don't assume that someone has glue unless you've sent it. Don't assume that someone has paper if you haven't sent it. I have been in many homes where there was neither book nor craft supply, so assuming that all families have both will likely mean that is a project that will not get done. When events are scheduled that require transportation, work with your district to partner with churches or community centers that have vans for use. Most will do this for free, but even if you provide gas or honorarium for their services, the benefit to the families can be huge.

John C. Maxwell is a *New York Times* best-selling author who has written books on topics ranging from spirituality to business leadership for the past 30+ years. He is world renowned for his ability to inspire and motivate others, empowering them to live more intentional lives. In a recent column, Maxwell discussed the need to create partnership when attempting to promote and accomplish larger goals. One of the things that he highlighted is how often, when attempting to create a tribe of loyal followers, you get only that, followers. When you are attempting to gather participants, partners, or mutually engaged team members, they must share the same passion and vision for the work needed to accomplish the goal. While it would be advantageous for all of our parents to walk into the classroom with the same zest for all of the necessary work involved in educating children, we don't have the luxury of choosing who we teach. When engaging reluctant parents, you have to consider the why behind their reluctance; another way to create partnership is by marketing the benefits of what you are trying to accomplish.

MARKETING YOUR PROGRAM

I know what you are thinking: You're an educator, not a public relations professional. No, I haven't taken leave of my faculties; I am about to talk about marketing. Most people think of marketing as simply commercials and other advertisements, but in reality, marketing is simply connecting with your ideal audience in an effort to elicit a desired response. Doesn't that sound like what we are trying to do? We know that parents are a valuable resource and we know that they can impact the outcome for students. We also know that they don't always see things the same way that we do. So, we're going to take a little help from the business world and connect on a different level. Beyond communicating effectively with parents, marketing allows you to connect with parents in a way that empowers and inspires you—a call to action that shows them value in the ideas that you are suggesting.

According to SBA.gov, the general principles of marketing are attracting and maintaining a large base of satisfied customers (U.S. Small Business Administration, 2015). For schools, that translates to determining the needs of our parents and satisfying those needs. These needs relate to products and services, promotion, price, and distribution. Schools might consider products and services things like homework and enrichment activities; promotion would be how we notify parents of these products, things like newsletters, social media posting, and phone communication. The price can be related to money, but most often this relates to the time and energy that parents invest in working with the kids on things like homework and projects.

Regardless of where you stand on the subject of school choice, takeovers, vouchers, charters, public schools or private, one of the best byproducts of all the discussion around school effectiveness is the engagement it sparks in parents as they listen to and participate in conversations about the education of their children. Because of that, we get to see a new development in schools—marketing.

How you market your program or school can depend on your funding, your mission, and the demographics of the families you are attempting to engage. In our communication chapter, we discuss how to use social media, written, and verbal methods of communication. A good marketing program for your school will likely include all of these items to some extent. Begin looking for ways to make the process smooth by asking families what they watch, where they shop, and the like. When you're doing it very well, you can also include cross-marketing that will encourage community members and stakeholders to value your school. Here's an example: When I was helping with the high school musical for one of my children, my task was meal prep. I was responsible for making sure that 48 hungry actors and actresses were nourished enough to practice into the night. Some of our meals were prepped by myself and other parents, but we also supplemented with food from a local restaurant. I had one parent tell me they liked a particular barbeque restaurant, so when I solicited them for funds, I said you're a school favorite. They were glad to support our production and supplied us with a meal with plenty of leftovers. By simply sharing what we were doing and knowing what our families enjoyed, the most natural partnership occurred. This is what marketing can do for your school.

DIFFERENT DOES NOT HAVE TO EQUAL DIFFICULT

As we end this section, I want to be clear on the idea that while we don't control anyone other than ourselves, we can create more difficult exchanges when we go into a scenario ready for battle. The biggest way to set yourself up to have a difficult conversation is to assume that it will be. Assume the best about parents, even when you have evidence to the contrary, so that you can communicate with them without the extra emotional baggage. Even when a parent has a direct complaint about you as an educator, you may feel like they are personally attacking your skill, integrity, or intentions. However, the complaint is not designed to prevent you from paying your mortgage. If you assume that every parent's goal is to have what is best for their children, attacking you is simply in defense of the one that they love. How far would you go to "protect" your child? I hear what you are saying: I am not the enemy; fighting me will not help the child. Focus on conveying that to the parent. They want to believe that

> The biggest way to set yourself up to have a difficult conversation is to assume that it will be.

and they may need you to prove it. During your most difficult parent interactions, ask yourself these three questions:

- What are they really feeling? Fear? Frustration? Guilt?
- What is an alternative version of my reality?
- What is my ultimate goal?

RELUCTANT EDUCATORS

I realized during the first draft of this book that I had not spent a great deal of time on reluctant educators. Because I know that many who read this will be working among other professionals with varying degrees of commitment to engaging all families, I close this chapter by spending some time on the subject of attracting allies within the school.

One of the experiences that I have thoroughly enjoyed is participating in the Equity Leaders Institutes sponsored by the Great Lakes Equity Center on the campus of Indiana University–Purdue University Indianapolis. During these two-day intensive workshops, educators from around the region come together to discuss how to improve equity practices in the schools we serve. It has been one of the most rewarding experiences of my career, as I sit among consultants, administrators, district leaders, state and national legislative committee members, and the like. Because we are likeminded in the desire to ensure more equitable distribution of resources, qualified staff, and legislative attention, the time spent together reinforces the feeling of not being alone in a very polarizing debate. Being in schools, you may not have this luxury on a daily basis. You may find yourself, on a good day, receiving blank stares when you talk about connecting more with families. Other days, you may be met with angry resistance from educators who believe their primary responsibility is the children and not the parents.

In my professional development sessions, working with Title I directors and administrators, I hear often that some teachers are doing well and others, not so much. When you are looking for an authentic collaboration, universal minimal standards are necessary so that all families receive similar services and no needs go unmet. The Equity Leaders Institute gives great direction for engaging reluctant participants or gaining allies.

The section on motivational interviewing can be applied to both parents and educators alike, but working in a shared format with fellow professionals may require some additional tools. Consider these agreements as a unique method of announcing the potential challenges of difficult conversations:

- *Stay engaged.* Whether you agree or not with what is being shared; stay involved.
- *Expect discomfort.* When you are having hard conversations, it's uncomfortable.
- *Speak YOUR truth.* Your viewpoint is important; please trust us enough to share.
- *Expect and accept nonclosure.* The issues we raise don't have simple solutions. We may not solve the world's problems, and sometimes a solution brings with it a whole new set of challenges; that's okay. This is a process (Singleton & Linton, 2006).

Vision

- Identify which tools are regularly in use at this time.
- Which skills do staff members most need to use?
- Of which categories of reluctant parents do you have the most?
- What are the reasons you have reluctant educators in your building?
- Like any good craftsman, using tools requires practice. Regular use of all the skills make the tools more effective. How can you implement regular practice to ensure that all staff members share a reasonable level of competency and comfort as it relates to the skills?

Plan

- Adding all the tools at once is unreasonable; how can you stagger exposure and practice time for staff?
- What professional development tools or trainings are needed to ensure adequate learning of all the tools?
- Are you able to establish a staff mentor program that would allow less experienced staff to share concerns without the fear of being penalized?

Action

- What methods can be used to progress monitor the family engagement?
- Having an outside assessment source can help reduce some of the pressure for internal staff "rating" colleagues.

(Continued)

(Continued)

Notes/Brainstorming

Putting It All Together 7

Life is a puzzle. Putting it together is the challenge.

—Anonymous

It is my sincere hope that in reading this book you will become passionate about engaging the families with whom you work. While I hope that working through the steps in this system will provide you with a formal written plan, my greater hope is that you will gain the valuable knowledge and insights to create significantly improved outcomes for the students in your communities.

Ultimately, a proper plan is only as good as the commitment of its participants, so I also hope that you have been inspired to actively pursue engagement on a daily basis by using a lens of family engagement at all times. In our final chapter together, we're going to look at a few programs that put these pieces together in an effective way.

So now you've done it. You've taken the time to investigate, create vision, plan, and take action. If you've done it well, the next year will be easier in some ways and in others seem more difficult. You will have more data with which to work, but then again, you will have more data with which to work. Growth is the key; sustainability is nonnegotiable.

One of the worst things that can happen in a parent-teacher organization is the dreaded graduation two-step. That's when you have one or two parents who are particularly passionate about the school and are strong school supporters, and then their children transition to the next school and you wonder what your school will do. This next section will help you take your efforts to the next level by looking at the ways you can branch out, experience growth, and fine tune the systems that you are already implementing.

INCLUDING AND EXPANDING THE COMMUNITY

It is completely unreasonable and unrealistic to believe that schools can provide all the necessary resources for families while trying to also educate their children. Combining resources with community-based organizations creates an optimal environment for supporting student success without overtaxing the professionals who are technically already overtaxed.

One of the things that I have noticed over the years is that there are nonprofit and government agencies for just about every need that can possibly arise. Many of them cease operations after a period of years because there is not enough awareness of the services that they offer to increase funding opportunities. Within each community, there are generally resources available that go unnoticed. When I teach the graduate counseling practicum class at the local university, I have my students do a "scavenger hunt" to identify five community resources located near their training sites. I have seen students find services from eating disorder clinics to food pantries. As a school, you want to be a hub of resources. Not only do I want parents and families to have confidence in my ability to educate their children, I also want them to have confidence in my commitment to supporting them in meeting any of their needs. Expanding the community means that you are actively seeking to include resources that will support the greater good of the school members.

CONFLICTS, CONFERENCES, AND MORE, OH MY!

It wouldn't be prudent of me to write an entire book about overcoming challenges to parent engagement and pretend that conflicts never occur. Even though you have this great roadmap for implementing engagement by practicing and encouraging families to participate, ultimately there will be times when bad things happen to good people. Whether the concern is a volunteer who oversteps his or her bounds and alienates other parents, or two adults who can't get along in the neighborhood bringing the conflict to the school, or even something as simple as hurt feelings when responsibilities get left undone, even the best engagement program will have problems that arise.

I had a very interesting conversation with a staff member at my school. She stated that when she called a mother to tell her that her son needed his asthma medication, that mom just "blew her off," stating that she was at work and her son would be fine. After another call, threatening to inform child protective services about the incident, the mom ended up bringing an expired prescription medication to the school. I got a referral to make contact with the family and offer assistance, with the potential need to make the report for medical neglect. When I got ahold of the mother, I had a completely different conversation than I expected. To my surprise, the mom had already sent in a new prescription directly to the nurse, which she picked up from the pharmacy after work the night before.

It's a classic example of miscommunication. Mom, perhaps, should have been more in tune with her son's medical needs, had the new prescription ready, or even been more agreeable during the phone conversation. However, it's also perfectly reasonable that a child with a chronic seasonal condition might run out of an infrequently used prescription. Being worried about missing work is a common concern for parents living at or below the poverty line and for some who live relatively comfortably in jobs that are highly competitive. Each hour missed could mean anything from something going unpaid to losing out on a promotion. Schools focused on supporting the family as the foundation of the child take all of these factors into consideration when communicating with parents or planning events. Sometimes, with really good intentions, we are ready for a fight with parents. We are passionate about the kids we serve and teach and we desperately want the parents on board, but if we're not careful, we can back them into a corner and the result usually leaves us all losing.

We've already talked about the importance of effective communication. I want to touch on it here as it relates to conflicts and not allowing them to derail your parent engagement efforts. Understanding that each individual perceives and delivers information through their own filter is a great place to start. In my work with families who are actively engaged in child protective services cases, you can imagine that there is plenty of room for conflict. While they are court ordered to participate in treatment with me, there is still much room for anger as I challenge them on things like parenting, budget, and relationship. I have been in more than one situation where, speaking as an officer of the court, I had to share information that was offensive to the parent. Taking time to put myself in their shoes helps me to hear things differently most times and also allows me to preempt major rifts.

You can also think of it as you might a close friend or family member. You can recall you and this person speaking at length about certain topics, perhaps even sharing experiences. Due to those shared experiences, you and your friend or family member will have a history, perhaps even "inside jokes," meaning other people can hear exactly what you said and not understand what you meant. This can work in your benefit. However, in other types of communication, particularly with someone with whom you share a limited connection or where there is already a conflict, the unspoken, yet potentially implied meaning of statements and actions can have very different results. Mastering the art of communication involves speaking in as clear a manner as possible with limited potential for misunderstanding, while also hearing and interpreting information from the other party in the same manner. Particularly when one feels misunderstood, or threatened, this can be even more difficult.

This is also true when working cross culturally or with families who have experienced traumas. It is unlikely that even the most culturally sensitive professional will be completely aware of every way in which a statement can be offensive, and walking on eggshells constantly is both impractical and counterproductive to the actual goals of our educational system. However, we do need to be considerate and look for ways to sharpen our tools and repair potential rifts in the alliances we are building.

See the set of examples below. Look for statements that could be interpreted in a negative way and then reframe them to be more clear and less potentially misunderstood. Pay attention to words and phrases that assume a shared understanding, phrases that are definitive, and comments that imply fault.

1. Johnny always has trouble getting started in the morning.

2. There seems to be a problem with the phone number you gave us.

3. Do you think you would be able to help him read after school?

4. I understand if finances are a problem; we have resources to help families.

Now, some of these were meant to be a little tricky and most I have heard before. The point I want you to understand is that communication is best experienced when there is a relationship. And when there is not a relationship, misunderstanding is more likely to occur than not occur. For statement one, "always" implies that there is never a time when this doesn't occur. That may be close to true, but it is unlikely that it is completely accurate. If I am a parent and hear that, I'm probably going to be looking, almost immediately, to prove you wrong with the one or two times when it was not. "Trouble" implies that there is a problem, with which the parents may or may not agree. A better way to say that might be, "I love having Johnny in my class. The afternoons go so smoothly that I'd like to help him transition from school to home a little more easily. Do you have any suggestions for me?" Yes, that statement is longer and might even take you extra mental effort to keep from using words or tones that could be met with hostility, but when there is already a conflict, or you fear one brewing, a few extra words can save you a lot of hassle.

For example two, the simplest way to say that is, "I think I have the wrong number for you." You could also say, "Is this the best number to reach you at during the school day?" I might even add, "My prep time is from 10:00–10:50 each day. Is it possible to reach you during that time?" All of these focus on the goal of getting the correct number without passing blame to the parent. Yes, ultimately we'd love them to give us the new numbers, but why start a battle when you don't have to? Another solution to this problem is to regularly update phone numbers and contact information with your class. Send home a contact info sheet and let every student who returns it get five extra minutes at recess. They will run home and beg their parents for the number, and you'll keep your records accurate.

Example three isn't too bad really, but if I can't read, do you think I'm going to tell you that? In this situation, I would say, "I think 10 minutes of extra reading time will help so much. He can do that with you or a sibling, even a babysitter." You could also ask parents if they read with the kids after school. Again, this is not a *bad* statement, just looking for ways of improving.

Example four is one of those that I put in just to trip you up a bit. It's exactly the type of statement that well-meaning social workers make every day, right before getting their head bitten off from parents who are embarrassed by the need for or offering of "charity." I based it off of the kind of comments that might come from a high school parent not wanting their child to apply to college or a parent who won't sign a field trip permission slip, but there are lots of times when family finances might come up. Recently, my school offered Christmas help to a family who, while not destitute by any means, was a large family and as deserving as any of our school families. Initially, the mother agreed to the assistance but then told me she changed her mind, saying that other people deserved it more. I don't know exactly why she ultimately declined, but I politely told her she was as deserving as anyone I knew and that I appreciated her honesty and generosity. I say that to share that you never know how a person might feel in certain situations or why they respond the way they do, but trying to understand can get you a long way. A less presumptive statement would be, "I don't want to impose, but can I ask if there is anything that we can do to assist with this?" Because federal legislation provides for free and reduced lunch, and the population qualifying for the assistance continues to increase, we sometimes lose sight of the fact that for some parents, limited financial resources can bring on feelings of shame or fear. I have had families existing with very little food because they are afraid that by asking they will set themselves up to be investigated or lose their children. This can go back to the empathy map we looked at in Chapter 2—to avoid conflicts, try and think about what your parents are thinking, feeling, and needing.

Here is a sample of the types of conversations that don't necessarily have easy answers. For this example, there is a student who has been referred to the counselor for self-harm, and now the parents must be notified.

You: Hello, Mr. Smith.

Parent: What did (student) do now?

You: I hope now is a good time to speak briefly. (Student) came to my office today and was a little concerned about being in trouble, but I explained that I was sure that you love her and want for her to be safe. She agreed with that and we decided to make the call.

Parent: Uh-huh.

You: Unfortunately, (student) has been having a tough time emotionally and has been harming herself. I'm so glad that today she is feeling courageous enough to trust me with this information and we know that including you is the best choice.

Parent: This is all for attention! There is nothing wrong with (student)! I have my hands full already. I don't have time for this!

You: I do understand. Parenting is so hard, and it can feel like we never get a break. Would it be ok if I offer a resource that I have found to be helpful? (Student) says that she doesn't want to make more work for you, but she knows that having a little extra time to talk would help. We have connections with a couple of agencies. Could I reach out to them and see if they have time to see (student)? It may take a few days, so in the meanwhile I'm going to send home a list of things that might help at home until we can get (student) in.

Parent: I don't have time to take her anywhere!

You: I understand. That's why they can meet with her right in this building. They can even come to your home if you like.

Parent: How much is that going to cost?

You: They do bill insurance, but let's cross that bridge a little later. Let's just start with this part and take it one step at a time. Would that work?

Parent: Okay, but I still don't think there's anything wrong.

You: You're right. You've got an amazing daughter. This can only help and I'm glad you're able to take care of this for her.

This was a tough one and, although this conversation ended well, there will likely be follow-ups that may not be as smooth. The goal is never perfection but always to first, do no harm and second, make progress as often as we can. Will this parent take me up on the offer for outside help? I don't know, but this is one step I can take today. Sometimes we wear ourselves out shooting for the "big picture" when we're in a difficult conversation or conflict. That can be very overwhelming and should be avoided.

Try as we might, there are times when no matter what we do, we cannot avoid the conflict. When that happens, first and foremost take a deep breath; conflicts are a perfectly natural byproduct of communication and relationship. Most are not relationship ending or dangerous in any way, and the biggest mistake that we can make is overreacting to what may actually be overreacting. When faced with a highly emotional person, remember your active listening and be aware of the communication tips that we focused on earlier in this book. The next step is to focus on finding a win-win solution.

The term "win-win" refers to resolving conflicts where both parties feel that they have won. For example, let's say that you have students refusing to do their reading log and you've asked the parents to help keep track by signing the log regularly. Unfortunately, the kids do their reading at the day care they attend while the mom works second shift, so not only is she not able to ensure that the reading occurs, by the time she picks the child up from day care at 11:30 p.m., she's not remotely concerned about the reading log at all. You've got a couple choices here. Anything from giving zeros for all the missing logs to forcing the student to miss recess every day to complete the logs might be well within your authority and even your rights, but how will either of those end with the student developing a love of reading, which is typically the goal of reading. But are there other solutions? Of course. What about contacting the parent and asking for her commitment to reading an hour each weekend rather than doing them during the week? What if you ask the mother to have the day care provider confirm the reading? Sure you don't necessarily get the parent directly involved, but having the student reading and confirmation of the reading is really a win all around.

In other scenarios, the win-win is less obvious. As a general rule, the older the child, the more freedom that they have to impact the outcome, so there are times when the school and the parent may have one request or desire and the student has another. Finding a win-win-win is still possible, but you have to focus on finding common ground. Let's use the example of a student who refuses to dress for gym class. The parents want them to dress but aren't going to come up to the high school every day and force them to change, and technically the student wants to graduate and understands the necessity in getting this credit. Focus on the common ground of knowing the class is required and that graduation is the goal. Work your way back to an amicable solution by finding out what is more important, in that moment, than these two agreed-upon facts. Sometimes you will find a deeper underlying root cause; other times you don't, but parents get to see you as an ally and may be more willing to follow through on discipline to reinforce what the school is trying to accomplish. Either way, starting with agreed-upon facts or working outward is much better than starting in the middle of a conflict and trying to find your way to the solution.

Some situations are trickier than others, and determining how to handle them is rarely a black-and-white issue. Looking at the following scenarios, consider how you might handle these situations. Practice them as a face-to-face, e-mail, or phone communication:

- A kindergarten student physically grabs the chest area of a female staff member and is met with a parent response that includes blaming the staffer for being too affectionate with her students.
- A parent wanted to send her fourth grader to military school and wanted the support of the school.
- The infant sibling of a student dies while the student was at school, and the parent wanted to know how to handle the situation.
- A parent calls to ask about literal "ants" in her son's pants.
- Parents think their child was doing well with no issues at all, and you are expected to break the news that the seven-year-old cannot spell their own name.
- You call home to tell a parent that your third-grade student is being defiant. They apologize and offer that they know she is having PMS since, at age eight, she has recently started having her period.
- A parent has e-mailed you stating that her daughter would not be bringing her backpack to school for several days because it was locked in her husband's car's trunk and the keys accidentally went with him to Afghanistan!

- You call home to explain to the parents of your student that he has been cursing in class. The mother, embarrassed by this behavior, shouts, cursing, to the husband, blaming him for the behavior.
- Parent tells you their child may have been possessed by a demon in the past that took his good behavior and speech.

PARENT-TEACHER CONFERENCE AGENDA

Having a step-by-step list is often helpful when there will be the potential for charged emotions in a meeting. While not necessarily needed for all parent and teacher conferences, particularly when there is a problem, an agenda can keep all participants on track. In Figure 7.1, there is a printable version of this form.

Here is the rationale behind the template.

Welcome and Introductions

The purpose of the welcome and introductions is to ensure that all parties are aware of current participants and roles. It is possible that participants will be in attendance where their roles have changed. For example, perhaps the mom had been staying home and was the primary provider of homework assistance and now, with her return to work, that assistance may be left to an older sibling or babysitter. Prior to the meeting, make sure families understand that anyone participating in the care of the child is welcome at the meeting. Some roles to consider are primary provider of transportation, primary assistant to homework or school work, primary provider of household routines, and the like.

Goals

While the goals of the meeting may be implied at the point of scheduling, viewing and/or clarifying goals at the beginning of the meeting can help if the meeting participants start to get off track. In closing the meeting, if goals have not been met, your action plan can be easily revised to include areas for further research or consideration.

Note: Other than for special education case conferences, which have legal requirements for topics to be discussed, having minimal goals for your meeting will ensure that it does not get out of hand or overwhelming for the family. For example, if a student has attendance issues, behavior issues, and academic issues, once you get the family into the meeting, it is not uncommon to try and

Figure 7.1 Parent Meeting Agenda

Meeting requested by _____ For (Student Name) _____

Attendees: _____

_____

2–5 minutes	**Welcome and Introductions**	Staff
2–5 minutes	**Goals**	Staff With Parent Input
5–10 minutes	**Ground Rules and Shared Expectations**	Staff and Family
5–10 minutes	**Family Story and Needs**	Parents
5–10 minutes	**School Story and Needs**	Teachers and Staff Members Present
5–10 minutes	**Brainstorming Solutions**	All Participants
2–5 minutes	**Action Plan**	All Participants
1–3 minutes	**Closing**	All Participants

Additional Instructions:

Action Step 1. _____ Assessment method _____

Accountable to _____ By _____

Action Step 2. _____ Assessment method _____

Accountable to _____ By _____

Action Step 3. _____ Assessment method _____

Accountable to _____ By _____

kill multiple birds with one stone. However, this can water down the effectiveness of the meeting. I suggest that, as a group, raise the concerns during the school story and needs portion of the meeting, but let goals be brought to the table. An example of a good goal is to improve a student's performance. The specifics of the family or school will determine the action plan.

Ground Rules and Shared Expectations

I suggest a preprinted list of ground rules or shared expectations. You can begin with some simple ones, such as we agree to table conversations that are not resolved and review them at a later time, or we agree to not raise our voices. Others might suggest only one person speaks at a time. Make sure to ask the family if they have any ground rules or expectations they would like to add.

Family Story and Needs

The family story can include current situations, needs, recent changes, or background information. A good conversation starter is, "Mr. or Ms. Jones, what would you like us to know about your family?"

Note: Some families may be uncomfortable with this type of starter. In that case, it is reasonable to start with the school story and needs. This can break the ice and get the ball rolling for communication.

School Story and Needs

With the challenges that many schools face in getting parents to the table to have a meeting, it wouldn't be uncommon to try and get everything out at once in case you don't get another chance. This method makes for a less productive meeting and typically increases the stress for all parties. Prior to the meeting, brainstorm to determine some positives that you can use for the "sandwich approach." Using the sandwich approach to the school story can be very helpful so that the meeting doesn't become a complaint fest. Start with one positive about the student, then list an area of concern, and end with another positive. See the following examples.

Positive: Jimmy is working so hard for Mrs. Smith. I can see the improvement in his math work.

Negative: He doesn't seem to be giving the same effort in his social studies class and I'm really worried about that grade.

Positive: I believe he has the ability to be really successful in all his classes.

Another example.

Positive: Tonya is such a pleasure to have in class.

Negative: However, her recent absences have really impacted her performance in science, as she has missed quite a bit of content.

Positive: With her hard work and improved attendance, I think she should be able to catch up by the end of the quarter.

Brainstorming

If you have done the story sections of the meeting correctly, brainstorming will come naturally. In the brainstorming section, the goal is to create a plan to address the negatives by building on the positives. See the below continuation of the sandwich approach examples we used in the school story section of the meeting.

1. *Problem:* A student's attendance is impacting his or her academic performance.

2. *Brainstorming questions:*
   - How much actual class time has been missed?
   - Is there any way to make up that time?
   - What other ways can the material that has been missed get delivered?
   - Is there room for extra credit or independent study?

Some solutions that might come up could include allowing the student to stay after school to make up the time that has been missed or even allowing him or her to prepare a presentation on an upcoming topic and share it with the class to show mastery. The goal of brainstorming is to *find* a solution, not to *convince* someone to take on your solution. It is fine for you to have an idea of what might work, but both parties need to be open to it. If you feel this would be a challenge, consider adding it to the list of ground rules.

Action Plan

This is the "who does what and when" of the meeting. Assigning tasks and deadlines creates the accountability that is needed to ensure change occurs.

Assessment Methods

We know progress monitoring is essential and accountability helps everyone. How will you measure whether this method is working or not? Establish these guidelines now so that everyone is on the same page.

Closing

End with a positive. I always thank parents for coming; a personal comment to any students present can also help.

Using the example of informing a parent about a Response to Intervention (RTI) referral, here is a sample script to give you an idea of some things to say.

1. Hello Mr./Mrs. (*parent name*), this is (*teacher name*), (*student name*)'s teacher.

2. I'd like to speak with you about some things I have noticed in class. Is now a good time?

3. A couple times per year, we check the students to see how they are doing in language and math. I am noticing that (*student name*) is not quite where we would like her or him to be, and I wanted to see if you are noticing some of the same concerns at home.

4. One of the things I would like to do to help here at school is start the RTI process. I can explain in more detail a little later, but basically it means that we will give (*student name*) more attention and help in language and/or math and keep a closer eye on his or her progress. Does that seem like something that would work for you?

5. The first thing we will do is have a meeting to discuss where he or she is and how long we want to monitor the progress. We can talk in more detail about some of the ways we will give them more help at school and some things you might be able to help with at home. Do you know your schedule for the next week? The meeting won't last too long, and we have a team of teachers who will join us to make sure we cover everything so that (*student name*) has everything that he or she needs.

6. Do you have any questions for me right now?

7. Great, we'll see you soon.

Possible Parent Questions

Why does my child need this?

We use standards or benchmarks to establish goals for all students that are closely linked with what the state says we need to meet. When we see kids who aren't matching the goal, we like to give them a little extra help to get them caught up to where they need to be.

What if I say no?

You have the right to accept or refuse any interventions because you are the parent; however, we do believe that this will be a benefit to your child. Do you have any specific concerns that we can address?

What if this doesn't work?

The process of monitoring and providing extra help can go on for the majority of the school year. However, if we see your child consistently not making progress or falling farther behind, we can move them up to getting more help or possibly test them for special education services.

A FINAL NOTE

Throughout this book, I have mentioned the creation of a formal parent engagement plan many times. While I continue to assert that it is an optional, yet highly effective, method of ensuring success in implementation, I wanted to make sure you have at least one sample of what this can look like.

Many schools include parent and family engagement under the general school improvement plan or Title I plans, which can help make sure that all staff members are regularly considering these topics. However, I prefer the separation of the plan in order to highlight it as a targeted focus. For your review, here is a basic sample engagement plan that includes what one school might look to include as the goals for engaging all families.

Sample Family Engagement Plan

The goal of the family engagement plan of (*school*) is to include families as partners in the holistic development of students at (*school*). The plan has the following goals:

1. Parents/Guardians will be welcome in the physical and figurative presence of (*school*) and are treated with respect in a friendly and helpful manner.

2. Parents/Guardians will be included as stakeholders in all leadership levels.

3. (*School*) will develop and implement a family and school compact as a part of this plan, which will describe the ways in which families, staff, and students share responsibility for improving student outcomes.

4. Families and educators will have the opportunity to provide input through surveys, web formats, and verbal exchanges.

5. Cultural, socioeconomic, language, disability, and demographic status will be directly attended to through the use of focus groups and advisory committees.

6. The school will provide opportunities for all families and students, including English Language Learners, to have the opportunity to provide input in regularly scheduled meetings of interest.

7. (*School*) will seek to consistently improve parent engagement by regularly conducting surveys to identify barriers to participation, improve effectiveness of strategies, and secure input on the quality of the plan.

8. Measurable goals for increasing the quantity and quality of family engagement will be included as a part of the school improvement and Title I plans.

9. The leadership of (*school*) will contribute financial and manpower resources toward increasing and supporting family engagement. (*School*) leadership commits to spend no less than 1 percent of annual Title I budget or (*insert $*) per year toward the successful implementation of the plan components.

10. (*School*) will provide professional development opportunities for staff to become better equipped at engaging families.

The following components will be directly addressed through the Family Engagement Plan.

Effective Parenting

1. Workshops will routinely be offered to promote effective and healthy parenting practices and will be facilitated by (*school*) with the support of professional community partners.

2. Materials and training will be provided to help parents work with their children to improve their achievement, such as literacy training and using technology to foster parent engagement.

3. Communication regarding student attendance will be delivered by multiple modalities, including verbal notification, written notification, and electronic notification.

4. (*School*) will model effective positive discipline and reward strategies by acknowledging good character, behavior, and academic performance of students.

5. Impression data will be taken anonymously from parents regarding participation in parenting workshops and presentations.

Effective Communication

1. All families will be notified of the family engagement plan in an understandable format, including translation into a language understood whenever possible.

2. (*School*) will hold at least one yearly meeting to present the family engagement plan and the rights of students and parents as assigned under the plan.

3. Workshops, groups, and events that are presented at (*school*) will be added to the family engagement calendar and all applicable school materials.

4. (*School*) accepts the responsibility in presenting information to parents on state and federal standards in the area of content, achievement, and local assessments and how to monitor and impact improvement.

5. Regular newsletter information will be presented to families in multiple formats and will include information on grade reports, test results, school programming, and suggestions for parent and family involvement.

6. Formal school conferences will be scheduled at a minimum of once per calendar year and can be requested at any time as needed by parents and/or teachers.

7. Curriculum and standards will be made readily available on the school website and upon request from teachers.

8. Parents will be provided with regular notice of, opportunity to attend, and input in meetings related to the education of their children.

9. Data for communication will be kept to document effectiveness of communication methods. These can include copies of material received as well as monitoring of electronic communication.

Volunteerism

1. (*School*) will maintain an open-door policy that supports parents being actively engaged in the school community through voluntary commitments. Whenever possible, these opportunities will be made available at no cost.

2. The staff of (*school*) will regularly provide parents with opportunities to volunteer both in and out of school toward enhancing the education of the student body.

3. (*School*) will provide or direct families to appropriate training programs to prepare them for engaging in volunteer activities.

4. Volunteers at (*school*) will regularly be recognized for their contribution to the school community.

5. (*School*) will support the development and recognition of family voluntary leaders.

6. Volunteer logs will be maintained to assess parent engagement in school activities.

Learning at Home

1. (*School*) will sponsor or present workshop events to promote effective learning practices at home. These can include math and literacy events, take-home activity packs, and interactive web-based programs.

2. Parent surveys will be conducted, via multiple modalities, at least once per year to determine supports needed for enhancing at-home learning.

3. (*School*) will regularly promote at-home learning by presenting strategies via multiple modalities. These can include being sent through paper or electronic newsletters, social media outlets, and at all school-sponsored events.

4. (*School*) will provide opportunities for parents to access and understand state and federal standards for curriculum and linkage to at-home learning.

Decision Making

1. The family engagement plan of (*school*) will make specific efforts to include parents as decision makers in the school setting. This can include holding positions on boards or subcommittees of boards.

2. Leadership of (*school*) will regularly seek opportunities to include parents and families in the process of decision making, including encouraging parents to be actively involved in the legislative process.

3. Parents and families will be allowed to submit proxy votes and contributions to school decisions without needing to be present for meetings.

Community Collaboration

1. (*School*) will partner with community organizations to support and enhance the academic, social, and emotional development of students and families.

2. As often as needed, community partners will be invited to participate in school events or share space within the school in order to provide ease of access for families.

References and Further Readings

All Pro Dad. (2015, November). About page. Retrieved from www.allprodad.com

Delgado Gaitan, C. (2004). *Involving Latino families in schools: Raising student achievement through home-school partnerships.* Thousand Oaks, CA: Corwin.

Ellison, G., Barker, A., & Kulasuriya, T. (2009). *Work and care: A study of modern parents.* Retrieved from http://www.equalityhumanrights.com/sites/default/files/documents/research/15._work_and_care_modern_parents_15_report.pdf

Engagement. (2015). In *Merriam-Webster's online dictionary* (11th ed.). Retrieved from http://www.merriam-webster.com/dictionary/engagement

Epstein, J. (2010). *School, family, and community partnerships: Preparing educators and improving schools.* Boulder, CO: Westview Press.

Forbes, H. (2012). *Help for Billy.* Boulder, CO: Beyond Consequences Institute.

Garst, K. (2015). *27 killer facebook post ideas for small business owners.* Retrieved from http://kimgarst.com/27-facebook-post-ideas/

Georiga Parent Mentor Partnership. (2015). Our mentors page. Retrieved from http://www.parentmentors.org/our-mentors/

Glasgow, N. A., & Whitney, P. J. (2009). *What successful schools do to involve families.* Thousand Oaks, CA: Corwin and the National Association of Secondary School Principals.

GoodTherapy.org. (2015). Active listening [Web log post]. Retrieved from www.goodtherapy.org: http://www.goodtherapy.org/blog/psychpedia/active-listening

Grant, K. B., & Ray, J. A. (2015). *Home, school, and community collaboration: Culturally responsive family engagement.* Thousand Oaks, CA: SAGE.

Great Lakes Equity Center. (2015). *Equity leaders institute educator retention fact sheet.* Indianapolis, IN: Author.

Kids Count Data Center, A Project of the Annie E. Casey Foundation. (2015). *Children in single-parent families by race* [Data set]. Retrieved from http://datacenter.kidscount.org/data/tables/107-children-in-single-parent-families-by#detailed/1/any/false/36,868,867,133,38/10,168,9,12,1,13,185/432,431

Lawson, M. (2003). School-family relations in context: Parent and teacher perceptions of parent involvement. *Urban Education, 38,* 77–130.

Lawson, M., & Alameda-Lawson, T. (2012). A case study of school-linked, collective parent engagement. *American Educational Research Journal, 49*, 651–684.

Livingston, G., & Cohn, D. (2010, August 19). *New demographic of American motherhood.* Retrieved from http://www.pewsocialtrends.org/files/2010/10/754-new-demography-of-motherhood.pdf

Logan Square Neighborhood Association. (2015). *Parent mentor program.* Retrieved from http://www.lsna.net/Issues-and-programs/Schools-and-Youth/Parent-Mentor-Program.html

Lopez, M. E., & Patton, C. (2013, December 5). Strengthening family engagement through teacher preparation and professional development. *FINE Newsletter, V(4).* Retrieved from http://www.hfrp.org/publications-resources/browse-our-publications/strengthening-family-engagement-through-teacher-preparation-and-professional-development

McInerny, C. (2014, May 6). Nine out of ten education referenda pass in Tuesday's election. *StateImpact Indiana, Education, From the Capitol to the Classroom.* Retrieved from http://indianapublicmedia.org/stateimpact/2014/05/06/ten-education-referenda-pass-tuesdays-election/

MetLife Foundation. (2007, November 19). *The MetLife survey of the American teacher: The homework experience.* Retrieved from https://www.metlife.com/assets/cao/contributions/foundation/american-teacher/metlife-survey-american-teacher-2007-homework-experience.pdf

MetLife Foundation. (2013, February). *The MetLife survey of the American teacher: Challenges for school leadership.* Retrieved from https://www.metlife.com/assets/cao/foundation/MetLife-Teacher-Survey-2012.pdf

Mirr, R. (2009). *Adapted Hoover-Dempsey & Sandler model of parental involvement: School/Teacher version questions.* Retrieved from http://www.nationalpirc.org/engagement_forum/resources.cgi?item=22

Mo, Y., & Singh, K. (2008). Parents' relationships and involvement: Effects on students' school engagement and performance. *Research in Middle Level Education Online, 31,* 9. Retrieved from http://files.eric.ed.gov/fulltext/EJ801108.pdf

National Center for Fathering. (2015, November). WATCH D.O.G.S. FAQs. Retrieved from http://www.fathers.com/watchdogs/watch-dogs-faqs/

National PTA. (2015). *National standards for family-school partnerships.* Retrieved http://www.pta.org/files/National_Standards.pdf

NBC News Education Nation. (2014). *State of parenting: A snapshot of today's families.* Retrieved from http://www.parenttoolkit.com/files/ParentingPoll_PrintedReport.pdf

O'Brien, A. (2015, August 5). *Making the most of back-to-school communications.* Retrieved from http://www.edutopia.org/blog/making-most-back-school-communications-anne-obrien?utm_source=SilverpopMailing&utm_medium=email&utm_campaign=082615%20enews%20fam%20ngm%20remainder&utm_content=&utm_term=fea3hed&spMailingID=12234370&spUserID=MTU3NzU0MDMwOTQ1S0

The Parent/Teacher Home Visit Project. (2011). *About the Parent/Teacher Home Visit Project.* Retrieved from http://www.pthvp.org/index.php/sacramento-region

PDK International. (2015). *PDK/Gallup poll of the public's attitudes toward the public schools: The 2015 PDK/Gallup poll report.* Retrieved from http://pdkpoll2015.pdkintl.org/

Relias Learning. (2014). *Motivational interviewing* [Online training course]. Retrieved from https://reliaslearning.com/courses/motivational-interviewing

Ridnouer, K. (2011). *Everyday engagement: Making students and parents your partners in learning* (p. 9). Alexandria, VA: ASCD.

Rose, C., & Smith, E. (2014, September 8). What school reform can learn from business: It's not what you think [Web log post]. Retrieved from http://engagingparentsinschool.edublogs.org/2014/09/08/guest-post-from-the-parentteacher-home-visit-project-what-school-reform-can-learn-from-business-its-not-what-you-think/

Rubin, C. M. (2015, June 16). The global search for education: Families, schools and communities. *HuffPost Education.* Retrieved from http://www.huffingtonpost.com/c-m-rubin/the-global-search-for-edu_b_7515792.html

Sears, J. (2015, December 31). Ring in the new year in the classroom [Web log post]. Retrieved from http://www.notsowimpyteacher.com

Singleton, G., & Linton, C. (2006). *Courageous conversations about race: A field guide for achieving equity in schools.* Thousand Oaks, CA: Corwin.

Taffel, R. (Accessed June 2015). *Helping today's parents: How to build a parent community.* Retrieved from http://www.psychotherapynetworker.org/

U.S. Department of Education. (2002, January 8). *No child left behind act of 2001.* Retrieved from http://www2.ed.gov/policy/elsec/leg/esea02/index.html

U.S. Department of Education. (2004, September 15). *Title I of the elementary and secondary education act of 1965.* Retrieved from http://www2.ed.gov/policy/elsec/leg/esea02/pg1.html

U.S. Department of Labor, Bureau of Labor Statistics. (2015, April 23). *Employment characteristics of families summary.* Retrieved from http://www.bls.gov/news.release/famee.nr0.htm

U.S. Small Business Administration. (2015, September). *Managing a business: Marketing 101.* Retrieved from https://www.sba.gov/content/marketing-101-basics

Wanless, S., & Patton, C. (2013, December 5). Professional development in family engagement: A few often-overlooked strategies for success. *FINE Newsletter, V(4).* Retrieved from http://www.hfrp.org/publications-resources/browse-our-publications/professional-development-in-family-engagement-a-few-often-overlooked-strategies-for-success

Watson, A. (2014, March). The logic behind the "illogical" mindset of students and families in poverty. *The Cornerstone.* Retrieved from http://thecornerstoneforteachers.com/2014/03/logic-behind-illogical-mindset-students-families-poverty.html

Weiss, H., & Lopez, M. E. (2009, May). Redefining family engagement in education. *FINE Newsletter, I(2).* Retrieved from http://www.hfrp.org/family-involvement/publications-resources/redefining-family-engagement-in-education

Index

Absenteeism, impact of culture on, 25–26
Accommodations, 57, 58
Active listening, 56–57, 125
ADHD (attention-deficit/hyperactivity disorder), 58
All Pro Dad, 30
Alternative education setting, 37–38
Americans with Disabilities Act (ADA; 1990), 33, 47
Applestein, Charlie, 36
At-home learning, 135–136
At-risk/challenging students, 35–37

Background checks, 51, 80, 96–97
Beststart.org, 29
Blended learning, 83
Body language, 57, 61, 62

Choice, school, 114
Collaborative care
   framework for, 52
   overview of, 5–8, 7 (figure)
Common Core, 2, 44, 58
Communication
   body language as, 57, 61, 62
   challenges, 61–62, 120–127
   family engagement plan and, 134–135
   terminology for, 57–58
   vocal tone and, 56–57, 61, 62, 65, 106, 122–123
   See also Communication strategies
Communication strategies, 55–73
   active listening, 56–57
   diversification of, 58–59
   electronic, 62–73
   e-mail, 61, 63–65, 63 (figure)–64 (figure)
   Facebook, 68–71
   MailChimp, 66–67
   newsletters (see Newsletters)

phone communication, 59–61, 114
social media, 67–73
Twitter, 71 (figure)–72
win-win solutions, 125–126
See also Communication
Community collaboration, 120, 136
Conferences. See Parent-teacher conference agenda
Cornerstone for Teachers, 31
Culture
   impact on absenteeism, 25–26
   overview of, 24–27
   visual/less visual components of, 25, 26 (figure)

Dads of Great Students (Watch D.O.G.S.), 30
Diary of a Not So Wimpy Teacher, 59

Early childhood learners, 39–40
Educator incentives, 88–89
Educators. See Teachers
Electronic communication, 62–73
   e-mail, 61, 63–65, 63 (figure)–64 (figure)
   newsletters, 65–67, 66 (figure), 136
Elementary and Secondary Education Act, 12
E-mail
   follow-up after phone call, 61
   tips for sending, 63–65, 63 (figure)–64 (figure)
   tone of, 65
Empathy map, 40–41 (figure), 43, 96, 124
Engagement, parent, 11–21
   current trends in, 19–21
   defining, 11–12
   educators' meanings of engaged parent, 49
   federal legislation on, 12–13

formal plan for, 132–136
framework for, 16 (figure)–17, 47, 79
historical data on benefits of, 16–19
involvement/participation vs.,
    14 (table)
parent involvement vs.,
    13–14 (table), 15
reluctant parents, 110–114
state legislation on, 13
See also Program, parent engagement
Enrichment activities, 43–44, 80,
    111, 114
Epstein, Joyce, 16 (figure)–17, 47
Equality and Human Rights
    Commission, 42
Equity Leaders Institutes, 116
Every Student Succeeds Act (2015), 13

Facebook, 68–71
Family Engagement Plan
    effective communication and, 134–135
    effective parenting and, 134
    newsletters and, 134, 136
    sample, 132–136
Family events, 90–95
    coordination of, 91
    planning guide, sample, 93 (figure)
    post-event data collection, 94–95
    pre-event strategy, 91
    schedule of, 91–94
Family First, 30
Fathers
    engaging, 28–30
    single, 28–29
FERPA regulations, 72
Financial instability of family, 30–31,
    113–114, 121
Flipped classroom, 64–65
Forbes, Heather, 36–37
Friday journal, 59

Gaitan, Concha D., 34
Georgia Parent Mentor Partners, 85
Goals of engagement, plan for, 50–52
Graduation rates, 17, 112

Harvard Family Research
    Project (HFRP), 83
Health and Wellness Night, 95
Henderson, Anne T., 17
Home visits, 104–109
    follow-up, 107
    funding for, 108

introductory letter, sample, 109
modeling and, 106–107
preparations for, 106
previsit contact with parents, 105
safety and, 107
staff training for, 108
teacher compensation for, 107
Homework, 27, 86, 102–103, 111, 112,
    114, 127
Hoover Dempsey and Sandler Model of
    Parent Engagement, 18

Iceberg model of culture, 25, 26 (figure)
Incentives
    educator, 88–89
    parent, 87–88
Individualized Education Plan (IEP),
    7, 33, 57, 103
Individuals with Disabilities Education
    Act (IDEA), 33, 47
In*Source Special Education Support, 47
Institutional assistant, 58
Interventions, defined, 57
Interviewing, motivational,
    101–103, 116
Involvement, parent
    engagement vs., 13–14 (table), 15
    framework for, 16 (figure)–17, 47, 79
    participation vs., 14 (table)

Jett, Pamela, 61

LaPlaza, 18
Lawson, Michael, 14, 20
Learning at home, 135–136
Liaisons, 86
Limited English language speakers,
    18, 33–34
    e-mailing and, 63 (figure)–64 (figure)
    family events and, 92, 94
    newsletters and, 65
Literacy Night, 95
Logan Square Neighborhood
    Association, 85
LRE (least restricted environment), 57

MailChimp, 66–67
Maslow's hierarchy of needs, 112
Math Night, 95
Maxwell, John C., 113–114
McVay, Susan, 108
Mental/physical illness in family,
    112–113

Mentor programs, parent, 83–85
MetLife survey, 43
Mirr, Ron, 18
Mo, Yun, 19–20
Modeling, 20, 29, 40, 89,
    90, 106–107
Motivational interviewing,
    101–103, 116

National PTA, 17
NBC News Education Nation, 1, 43
Needs assessment, 76–80,
    77 (figure)–79 (figure)
"The New Demographic of American
    Motherhood," 35
Newsletters
    as marketing tools, 114
    at-home learning and, 136
    electronic, 65–67, 136
    Family Engagement Plans and,
        134, 136
    highlighting families in, 99
    highlighting volunteers in, 98
    older parents and, 37
    Smore sample, 66 (figure)
No Child Left Behind Act (NCLB; 1999),
    12–13, 57
"Not Everyone Was Raised in Your
    House," 61

O'Brien, Anne, 58–59, 64–65
Older parents, 37
Open house/open door hours, 95

Parent engagement program, components
    of, 75–99
    background checks for volunteers,
        51, 80, 96–97
    educator incentives, 88–89
    family events, 90–95
    intentional incentives, 87–88
    intentional professional development,
        80, 82 (figure)–83
    parent mentor programs, 83–85
    parent nights, 89–90, 95
    parent open house/open
        door hours, 95
    parent resource center, 86
    recognition/rewards, 98–99
    take-home family activity packs,
        90, 135
    volunteer training/acknowledgment,
        97–98

Parents
    as ill-equipped to support schools, 2
    current research on, 42–44
    empathy map, 40–41 (figure),
        43, 96, 124
    fathers, 28–30
    liaisons for, 86
    living in poverty, 30–31,
        113–114, 121
    of at-risk/challenging students, 35–37
    of early childhood learners, 39–40
    of students in alternative education
        setting, 37–38
    of students receiving special education
        services, 32–33
    older parents, 37
    participation by, 14 (table)
    single parents, 27–28
    survey, 44–45, 46 (figure)
    types of, 23–24, 27–40
    vignette about caring/minimally
        involved parents, 2–4
    what parents want, 45, 47
    with limited education, 112
    with limited English language (see
        Limited English language speakers)
    working parents, 27
    young parents, 34–35
    See also Engagement, parent;
        Involvement, parent; Parent
        engagement program,
        components of
Parent-teacher conference agenda,
    127–132
    action plan, 130
    assessment methods, 131
    brainstorming, 130
    closing, 131
    communication issues, 120–127
    family story and needs, 129
    goals, 127, 129
    ground rules, 129
    possible parent questions, 132
    school story and needs, 129–130
    template, sample, 128 (figure)
    welcome/introductions, 127
Parent/Teacher Home Visit Project,
    104–105, 107
Participation, vs. involvement/
    engagement, 14 (table)
Payne, Ruby, 30–31
PDK/Gallop Poll, 44
People-first language, 24

Phone communication
for marketing engagement
program, 114
tips for, 59–61
Positive reinforcement, 40, 110
Poverty, 30–31, 113–114, 121
"Poverty Impedes Cognitive Function," 32
Professional development
intentional, 80, 82 (figure)–83
needs assessment for, 76–80,
77 (figure)–79 (figure)
Program, parent engagement
funding of, 96
marketing of, 114–115
needs assessment for, 76–80,
77 (figure)–79 (figure)
supplies/materials for, 97

Reflective listening. *See* Active listening
Reinforcement, positive, 40, 110
Resource center, parent, 86
Ridnouer, Katy, 14
Rollins, S. Kwesi, 11–12

Sandwich approach, 60, 129–130
School choice, 114
School counselor, 58
School improvement program, 52, 132
School psychologist, 58
Science Night, 95
Services Learning Night, 95
Singh, Kusum, 19–20
Single fathers, 28–29
Single parents, 27–28
Smore.com, 65–66 (figure)
Social media, 67–73
Facebook, 68–71
for marketing engagement program,
114, 115
parents nights and, 89–90
template for posts, 69–71
Twitter, 71 (figure)–72
See also Communication; E-mail

Special education services
parent-teacher conferences and,
127, 129
students receiving, 32–33
St. Mary's Children's Center,
32, 39 (figure)–40

Take-home activity packs, 90, 135
Teachers
challenges to, 4–5
job satisfaction and, 16
needs assessment, 76–80
reluctant, 116–117
See also Professional development
Thank-you cards, 98, 107
Title I of ESEA, 12, 86, 116, 132
Tone of voice, 56–57, 61, 62, 65, 106,
122–123
Traditional education model, 111
Tutoring programs for students, 112
Twitter, 71–72
hashtag tool for, 72
profile, sample, 71 (figure)

Vision, 10, 50, 51, 52, 87.114
Vision, Plan, Action (VPA), 5, 8
Vocal tone, 56–57, 61, 62, 65, 106,
122–123
Volunteers, 80, 84, 135
background checks for,
51, 80, 96–97
bookmarks for, sample, 81 (figure)
for family events, 92
recognition/rewards for, 98–99
training/acknowledgment of,
97–98

Watch D.O.G.S. (Dads of Great
Students), 30
Watson, Angela, 31, 32
Working parents, 27

Young parents, 34–35

A SAGE Publishing Company

Helping educators make the greatest impact

CORWIN HAS ONE MISSION: to enhance education through intentional professional learning.

We build long-term relationships with our authors, educators, clients, and associations who partner with us to develop and continuously improve the best evidence-based practices that establish and support lifelong learning.

Solutions you want. Experts you trust. Results you need.

AUTHOR CONSULTING

Author Consulting

On-site professional learning with sustainable results! Let us help you design a professional learning plan to meet the unique needs of your school or district. www.corwin.com/pd

INSTITUTES

Institutes

Corwin Institutes provide collaborative learning experiences that equip your team with tools and action plans ready for immediate implementation. www.corwin.com/institutes

ECOURSES

eCourses

Practical, flexible online professional learning designed to let you go at your own pace. www.corwin.com/ecourses

READ2EARN

Read2Earn

Did you know you can earn graduate credit for reading this book? Find out how: www.corwin.com/read2earn

Contact an account manager at (800) 831-6640 or visit **www.corwin.com** for more information.